CONTENT

C000174496

Next Parish America

Goleen Past and Present

Compiled and edited by
Denis Downey on behalf of
Goleen & District Community Council

Published by
Goleen & District Community Council

Photo credits:
Mary Hayes, Dr. Brian O'Connell, Tom Bullock, CJ Thomas, Sue Hill

Design and print by Inspire, Skibbereen, County Cork, Ireland.
Printed in Ireland.

ISBN: 978-0-9557428-0-4

ACKNOWLEDGEMENTS

The Goleen Community Council would like to thank everybody who helped in various different ways with the writing and completion of this book on our parish history past and present. A very special word of thanks is due to the following, who wrote articles: Paul O'Sullivan, chairman of the Community Council, Denis Downey, Michael Collins, Michael McCarthy, Betty Barry, Jim O'Meara, Sue Hill, Geraldine Camier, Ellen Scully, Mary Sheehan, Kieran O'Sullivan, Billy O'Sullivan and Jerry O'Mahony, Neillie O'Sullivan, Breda Buckley, Eamonn Sheehan, Michael O'Reilly, Connie O'Driscoll, Claire Barrett, Denis O'Neill, Jo Kerrigan and Richard T Mills. A debt of gratitude is also due to the following individuals and organisations who helped in various ways: Mizen Archaeological and Historical Society; *The Southern Star*; Skibbereen Heritage Centre; The Central Statistics Office, Cork; Census Department, Swords, Co Dublin; The Heritage Council; Paddy O'Sullivan and Edward Bourke, Michael Sexton, Cork County Council, Skibbereen; Eileen Coughlan, Pat McCarthy, Stephen O'Sullivan, Denny O'Meara, Aidan Power and Geraldine Downey, who typed all the various articles for *The Southern Star*.

FOREWORD

It is said that every townland or village in the country has its own story to tell. This is certainly true of the part of the Mizen peninsula covered by Goleen and District Community Council, which comprises the parish of Goleen with its 92 townlands stretching from Dunbeacon and Lowertown in the east, to Crookhaven and Mizen Head in the west.

The parish of Goleen contains Mizen Head which is Ireland's most south-westerly point. What with its rugged coastline and its many recorded shipwrecks, the eleven piers and two lighthouses which saved many a boat with their guiding lights, one would have just enough to fill a book on this alone. However, there is much more to Goleen that just its coast. One has only to look at the picturesque villages of Toormore, Goleen and Crookhaven, which are popular holiday destinations for those from near and far, the unique Mizen Visitors Centre at Mizen Head, the histories of the churches, both Roman Catholic and Church of Ireland, and the Goleen Parish Newsletters for each of its 92 townlands, to see that Goleen and its environs is teeming with history that should be remembered and cherished.

However, any parish or area's most important asset is its people and it is the people that ensure that an area continues to thrive or prosper. It is for this reason that this book also tries to convey a picture of modern-day life in the Goleen area. This can be seen through its voluntary organisations, such as Goleen IFA, Goleen Community Playgroup and Goleen Parish Hall, its sporting bodies, such as Goleen GAA and Mizen AFC, and, most recently in the past few years, the development of the new Community Sports Complex at Boulysallagh on the outskirts of Goleen village.

This book does not seek to be an exhaustive account of everything that has taken place in the Goleen and district area, either in the past or at present, nor does it seek to purport that those organisations whose histories are not recounted herein are not as equally important or worthwhile as the articles that have been included. Much valuable material had to be excluded due to pressure of space. Neither does this book purport to be a scholarly work penned by an eminent historian. What it does hope to do is to collate a history of the Goleen and district area including some articles previously published elsewhere so that both local and stranger to the area can have a reference point in respect of the history of our area and, most importantly, so that recollections of our older generations are preserved for future generations.

We have sought to give each facet of our history and of our community its share of coverage in this book and we have tried to ensure that all information contained is accurate and correct so far as possible. Any inaccuracies herein have been made in good faith and we hope that they will be accepted as such by readers of this book.

I would like to thank all those who have contributed articles to this book for their time and assistance,   to Denis Downey for compiling and editing the book and *The Southern Star* for printing of same. Most of all, however, I would like to thank Denis Downey, a member of our Community Council, who first proposed the idea of putting a book together at a Community Council meeting and who has pursued this project with unstinting hard work and perseverance thereafter.

Finally, I hope this book on Goleen's past and present will have something of interest for everyone and that it may lead to a greater awareness of the rich heritage and history of our area. While we as a community must always strive to improve, modernise and develop our area so that it reaches its full potential, it is equally as important that we cherish and remember our past.

Paul O'Sullivan
Chairperson,
Goleen and District Community Council

OUR PARISH

by Denis Downey

Goleen is the most south-western parish in Ireland and is known to have one of the most rugged and scenic coastlines in the country. It is a reasonably large parish with 92 townlands stretching from where the river enters into Crew Bay at Lowertown to where the river enters the sea at the townland of Drishane in Dunbeacon.

The parish has roughly 30 miles of coastline which has eleven piers listed with Cork County Council and they are as follows: (64) Kilcomane, (65) Dunmanus Pier, (66) Canty's Cove, (67) Gortdubh 'Doonee Coos', (68) Toor, (69) Dunlough, (70) Corran, (71) Crookhaven, (72) Goleen, (73) Goleen, (74) Coosaphuca. That coastline has two lighthouses, Mizen Head and Rock Island, three lookout towers in the townlands of Cloughane, Brow Head and Leamcon. The largest townland is Rathura with 1,183 acres and the smallest is Clogher with 33 acres.

Fifty-five townlands are coastal. One of the highest mountains is Caher, sometimes referred to as the Mizen Peak. In a rock at the top of Caher hill is a footprint which local lore says was made by a priest fleeing from the pursuing redcoats. This place is known as the Priest's Leap. A small well at this place is known locally as Bolair and the waters of which are said to have properties to cure warts. In graves at the west side are the remains of sailors whose bodies were washed ashore in the distant past. There is what's known as a Cairn on its peak. Other Cairns can be found on its slopes. Also on its southern side is the coastguard station, which was guarded round the clock during the last century until the mid-1940s. One of the last coastguards who served there is still living.

A short distance from the coastguard hut is marked the letters E I R E with flagstones, which were for identification purposes for aircraft during the wars. The marks of white paintings on the flagstones are still visible. On the southern side of the mountain is a children's burial ground. The southern side of Caher hill may have been guarded by a lighthouse, a lookout tower and the coastguard station but at the foot of its northern side it was guarded for 107 years by the late Tom Barry, who, for the last two and a half years before his death in 2003, was the oldest male citizen in Ireland.

Lissigriffin lakes are the largest lakes in the parish and 50 years ago were renewed for their trout fishing and were also home to some 200 swans. The townland of Ardeavinna has a standing stone (*galán*) and a 'portal dolmen', the only one of its type in the parish. In Lissacaha, there is a triple-fossed ring fort, the largest of its kind in West Cork. There is evidence of a *fulachta fiadh* (an Ancient cooking place), which was found in recent times in the northern side of the townland, and in the eastern side of the townland is a pound field 'used in the last century'. In Cove Strand are the ruins of an old lime kiln and there are copper mines in several townlands in the parish.

The parish has two Roman Catholic churches, St Patrick's Church in Goleen and the Church of the Seven Sacraments in Lowertown. There are two Church of Ireland churches in the parish – St Brendan's, Crookhaven, which is open for monthly evening services and weddings. The Church of Ireland in Goleen closed for religious services on 30th June 1991. The Altar Church is the main Church of Ireland for religious services. There are two national schools open in the parish, Lissigriffin and Goleen. There is one priest in the parish and a Rector living at the Altar. The parish has a resident doctor and one garda, a TD, one member of Cork County Council and one member of Community and Voluntary Forum.

There are eight licensed premises in the parish – four in Goleen village, three in Crookhaven and Barleycove Hotel. There are three post offices in the parish – Crookhaven, Goleen and Toormore. There is one grocer shop and restaurant in Crookhaven. There is a grocer shop in Toormore. In Goleen there are two grocer shops, fast food shop, restaurant, butcher shop, green grocer shop, petrol station, craft shop, art gallery, a new medical centre, children's playground and children's playgroup centre, parish hall, garda station, coast life-saving centre, a new community playing field and state-of-the-art sports hall. All of these are situated within walking distance of the village.

There is a very active community council with sixteen elected members, GAA Club, Soccer Club, Road Bowling Club, Horse Racing Committee, ICA, IFA, Children's Playgroup, Cliff Rescue Service, Inshore Boat Rescue Service, Community Alert Group, Community Care Group, St Joseph's Young Priests Society, PTAA and Hall Committee, all working for the sporting, caring and safety of the parish.

There are two creamery stores run by Drinagh Co-Operative, one in Goleen and one at Lowertown. There is a visitor centre and restaurant at Mizen Head; a hotel, restaurant and bar at Barleycove; a caravan site at Crookhaven, which also has its own shop and play area including a tennis court, and Crookhaven Sailing Club. There are castles, lookout towers, ring forts, mines, mass rocks, holy wells, wedge tomb, old church ruins, cairns and children's burial grounds scattered throughout the parish.

Much detail of many of the above clubs, committees and organisations will be found inside the pages of this book. I hope you will enjoy reading about our parish past and present and I would like to thank the many people who wrote on the various articles, also the many who gave information on various articles and others who gave permission to copy from their own books and journals. Much of the history and information of the various townlands of the parish were published in the weekly newsletters composed by that great historian the late Michael R O'Donovan, RIP, the first of the 92 newsletters were published on 20th April 1997 and were completed two years later.

The following article entitled 'Aspects of Goleen Parish Past and Present' was also written by Michael and is giving a history of the parish from the *fulachta fiadh* to the present times. We are grateful to his wife Margaret and family for permission to print same.

Festival Committee

ASPECTS OF GOLEEN PARISH, PAST AND PRESENT

by the late Michael R O'Donovan

Goleen parish is the most southerly parish in Ireland and is one of 57 parishes in the Diocese of Cork. It has a total of 92 townlands both large and small. In the old civil records, it is described as Kilmoe and West Skull.

The earliest evidence for the presence of man in the parish is found in the *fulachta fiadh* in the area. These belong to the time when man was a hunter gatherer. He hunted wild animals, cooked them in the *fulachta fiadh* (ancient cooking place) and moved on. These sites are difficult to date due to lack of dateable material, but similar sites excavated in Co Offaly gave a date of 8500 BC.

The Bronze Age is well represented in the parish where there are no less than eleven megalithic tombs. These are in the townlands of Ardervinny, Rathooragh, Alter, Toormore, Ballyrisode, Ballydevlin, Ballyvogue, Ardslough, Tooreen, Letter and Dunmanus. Carbon dating from two sites excavated gave a date of 1100–1300 BC. The discovery of a Bronze Age axe at the Toormore site was of considerable interest.

The megalithic tomb in the townland of Alter is the only archaeological site in the Mizen peninsula and is in State care (Dúchas).

The early Christian period is represented in the number of ancient cemeteries present. These are interspersed throughout the parish, many with foundations or ruins of an early church or oratory.

In many instances, townland names indicate the association of a saint or holy person with that place, i.e., Cill Cheangail, Kilmore, Kilbrown, Kilbarry, Kilpatrick, Kilcommon, Killeane. The existing church ruins of Kilmoe and Cill Cheangail are early medieval in architecture, but are possibly built on an earlier Christian site.

Many holy wells are in the parish – some dedicated to various saints, where, on the saint's feast day, various religious practices were observed. The practices are no longer in use. Some wells had properties to cure various ailments, such as eye problems, warts and depression. Many of the wells are now difficult to define as such, as they are infilled with silt with the passage of time.

Dúns, Liosanna, agus Rathanna abound in the parish. The former date to the Iron Age and were mainly defensive and built on the coast. Ráth and Liss were the first farmer settlements. The farmer and his family lived in huts within the enclosure, which also accommodated his livestock.

The bank and ditch which surrounded the *lios* were protective rather than defensive. Protection was necessary from wild animals that lived in the forests and from raiders. These sites are some of the best-preserved archaeological sites in the parish and also the most numerous. They belong mainly to the early Christian period.

The O'Mahony clan were the most dominant clan in the parish from the 13th to the sixteenth century. The remains of many of those castles are still visible. Those are at Leamcon, Dunlough and Dunmanus. Four others which stood at Dunkelly, Castlemehigan, Crookhaven and Ballydevlin are now gone. The O'Mahony clan took an active part in the 1641 rebellion which resulted in the forfeiture of their lands. The land was subsequently given to Cromwellian adventurers and English planters, who became the new landlords. Many of the big houses of the landlord era can still be seen, e.g., Hulls, Notters, Hungerfords and Flemings. The landlords are long gone and the big houses are now holiday homes.

The Great Famine, 1845–1848, had a devastating effect on the parish. This is reflected in the sharp decline in the population in the years 1841–1851. In 1841, the parish population was 12,045, which was reduced to 6,611 in 1851 – a loss of over 6,000 persons due to famine, disease and emigration. A number of facts contributed to that situation: the high population density and grinding poverty; the almost total dependence on the potato for food; the indifference of the English authorities, who could have done so much in the early stages of the Famine, but failed to act. The grim reminders of that time can be seen in the famine pits in local cemeteries, in isolated graves on the hillsides and in the undug potato ridges in some isolated places – left untouched when the potatoes rotted.

During the Napoleonic wars, a series of signal towers was built along the south and west coasts of Ireland. Goleen parish is possibly the only parish in Ireland with three signal towers, all of which are intact. The towers were garrisoned for short periods and were abandoned early in the nineteenth century when the threat of invasion has passed.

The sea played an important part in the life of the parish, as it does for all coastal communities. It provided sand and seaweed necessary as a fertiliser. To supplement the sand, which was often low in calcium carbonate, limestone was brought by boat and burned in kilns erected on the shore before being applied to the land. The remains of the kilns can be seen at Cove and Ballydevlin.

Part-time fishing was a useful source of food and income, and many small farmers had their own boats, which were kept in sheltered strands or hauled ashore in winter time. A large number of small piers provided access to the sea and safe moorings. These were situated at Kilthomane, Dunmanus, Dunkelly, Gortdubh, Cloghane, Corran, Crookhaven, Rock Island, Leenane, Goleen, Ballydevlin and Castlepoint. In the seventeenth century, pilchard fishing was developed in the parish by the Hulls of Leamcon, with Boyle and Roper as partners. The remains of pilchard presses can be seen at Leamcon, Crookhaven, Leenane and Dunbeacon. The presses were used to extract the oil before curing the fish.

In the 19th and 20th centuries, seine fishing was highly developed, particularly in the Dunmanus and Dunkelly areas. This was a source of much employment, as, in addition to the seine crews, scores of people were employed in curing, salting and barrelling the fish. Boat building and repair facilities were situated at Rock Island and Toormore. Today, the fishing tradition in the parish is maintained with boats operating mainly from Dunmanus, Crookhaven and Goleen, and a small fish-processing unit is in place at Rock Island.

Today, the population of the parish is slightly under 1,000, a dramatic decline from all-time record of over 12,000 in 1841. Nevertheless, it is both vibrant and progressive. Many of the small farms have disappeared, absorbed into larger units, which are efficiently run and well serviced. The natural beauty of the parish, its sandy beaches, rugged terrain and remoteness from the mainstream of life, are perhaps its greatest assets.

Hundreds of holiday homes are now built and thousands come for holidays in summertime, when the population increases almost fourfold. This is of considerable benefit to the services sector and employment in general. Crookhaven and Goleen are the commercial and socialising centres for both locals and tourists. In former times, Crookhaven was the hub of the news world, when both Lloyds and Marconi had centres there. Today it is frequented by yachtsmen from many parts of the world. The Mizen area is home to many species of rare plants, and large colonies of sea birds nest in the nearby cliffs. Much of the history, wildlife and marine biology of the area is captured in the Mizen Interpretative Centre, situated on the rocky promontory that was formerly the Mizen lighthouse.

Note: This article was written by the late Michael R O'Donovan and published by *Mizen Journal*.

To an outsider having watched these tractors at work they would expect a good crop of barley in the autumn but instead it has turned out to be a fine playing field which hosted the West Cork Junior 1 football semi-final between Muinter Bhaire and Caheragh.

GOLEEN AND DISTRICT COMMUNITY COUNCIL

by Michael Collins

Since the break-up of Muintir na Tire Group in Goleen in the early 1960s, there was a strong feeling that Goleen needed a group that could represent the whole community. In 1999, a steering group was set up to form a Community Council. Election papers were sent to every person in the parish over the age of 18. The area was divided into eight constituencies, each consisting of approximately 120 in population in each constituency. 'Area A' being Cahir, Barleycove to Toor; 'Area B' – Crookhaven, Leenane, Letter; 'Area C' – Goleen Town, Boullasallagh; 'Area D' – Dunkelly, Gorthduv, Kilbrown; 'Area E' – Ballydevlin, Enoughter, Kealfadda; 'Area F' – Dunmanus, Toormore, Knockeens; 'Area G' – Lowertown, Leamcon, Gunpoint; 'Area H' – Rathoora, Ardravinna, Dunbeacon.

Firstly, people had the chance to vote for anyone in their area and, when these votes were counted, the people with the six highest amounts of votes were eligible to go forward. The papers were then distributed once again with only six names on them and all had the opportunity to vote for two out of the six. These papers were again counted and the two with the highest votes were then elected to represent the people of their area for three years. In 1999, the first elected were: 'Area A', Pauline Reidy and Joe Hurley; 'Area B', Anthony O'Callaghan and Therese Laycock; 'Area C', Brian O'Connell and Gerard O'Donovan; 'Area D', Irene Cullinane and Pat McCarthy; 'Area E', Billy Connell and Sue Hill; 'Area F', Derry Kennedy and Betty Johnson; 'Area G', Michael Collins and Mary O'Callaghan; 'Area H', Eleanor Bowen, John O'Driscoll and Patrick Kennedy. Co-opted on to the Community Council was Tim Sheehan, Connie O'Driscoll, Ellie O'Leary, Denis Downey, Geoff Cutler, Rose O'Sullivan, Joe Notter, Sean Barry, Sylvia Connell and Owen Kelly.

This newly formed Community Council worked hard for the first three years, taking on projects such as a Needs Survey compiled for the parish, which clearly indicated that roads were a huge problem in the area; they also created a development plan for the Goleen parish; a playground for the children, where £10,000 was successfully raised in the community; entered Goleen in the Tidy Towns Competition; started a summer festival; got a grapevine newsletter up and running; started negotiations on the re-opening of an old pathway by the church in Goleen; safeguarded the future of the Toormore telephone box; started their own website; helped negotiate the pontoon development in Barleycove; funded works at McClean Grotto in Lowertown; succeeded in getting a new water pipe laid down from the reservoir to Goleen Cross; and gave every child in the parish a millenium medal and a biro to mark the millienium.

After these and many more projects were completed to 2002, with the three years up, it was time for another election, and elected this time were: Joe Hurley, Denis Downey, Anthony O'Callaghan, Maureen Newman, Brian O'Connell, Geraldine Camier, Ellen Scully, Maurice Couglan, Sue Hill, Eamon Sheehan, Tom Jermyn, Paul O'Sullivan, Mary Lucey, Tim Barnett, Michael Collins and Connie O'Driscoll. This committee followed on with the good work that the previous community council had done. They succeeded in getting a can recycling bank for Goleen; started up the now hugely successful local lotto; in early 2002, identified ground for a community centre in Boullasallagh; sought unsuccessfully to have Southdoc based in Schull Hospital to serve the people of the Mizen peninsula; organised a 2 o'clock bus for the young children in the Lowertown area; co-funded a slipway in Toormore and co-funded the graveyard improvements in Dunbeacon; funded the entrance walls to Goleen; supported the planning application for the Lowertown Nursing Home and East End Hotel; got a local house-to-house refuse collection started; helped get speed restriction signs in Crookhaven; helped out in the Mizen Rovers Soccer Club and the Gabriel Rangers ladies' football fundraisers; funded the Kilmoe carpark extension; succeeded in getting the rural bus to Goleen two times weekly; co-funded the public lighting in Toormore Church; collected all over West Cork and all over the world for our community centre; got Rathoora Cross widened; put together the new development plan; succeeded in getting the bad bends in Toormore straightened; got mobile mast erected in the Brow Head for better mobile reception in the parish; got three new 5,000-gallon tanks erected in Lowertown to help out in the water crisis; got Coorlacka Road widened and resurfaced; started off the Rural Social Scheme where we now have five workers working on the scheme; and

succeeded in getting double yellow lines at Ballyrisode to ease the
traffic problems there.

At the end of this three-year term, it was back to the people of the
parish to elect a new committee. Elected this time were: Joe Hurley,
Denis Downey, Maureen Newman, Anthony O'Callaghan, Geraldine
Camier, Vikki Evans, Ellen Scully, Pat McCarthy, Sue Hill, Eamon
Sheehan, Tom Jermyn, Paul O'Sullivan, Denis O'Neill, Tim Barnett,
Michael Collins and Connie O'Driscoll. These had to continue the
good work done by the last committee. The new committee started
with coastal erosion in Castlepoint pier with access steps for the public erected; a Goleen combined dinner dance was organised; Urban
Village Grants were granted, with Goleen getting €9,000 for public
lights; Lowertown got €7,000 for a wall-building project; Toormore
got €7,000 for a wall-building project; Dunbeacon Action Group got
€6,000 for a creamery stand; the committee co-funded the Toormore
wall-building project; co-funded the public lighting around the community centre; got bad bends removed in Cahir; bends removed in the
Lowertown and Cove Coast Road; helped out in the Goleen creamery
crisis; succeeded in getting the Mizen Road widened; succeeded to get
the extremely bad bend at Cashelane removed; helped out in resolv-
ing the ongoing Dunbeacon bus saga; lobbied successfully in getting
an area engineer appointed to Schull; co-funded and succeeded in getting grant aid for public lighting in Goleen, costing €15,000; ran the
yearly festival and had a 'Mayor Contest' that Denis Downey won.

A new sub-committee formed was 'Faith Matters', dealing with the
possibility of having no priest in the parish. After some dialogue with
the Bishop John Buckley of Cork, he appointed Fr John O'Donovan to
the parish. We co-funded public lighting in Crookhaven; got urban
village renewal, Clar, and Leader money for Lowertown and Goleen;
and succeeded after a long struggle in getting broadband to the com-
munity.In the past eight years we have been extremely busy. We have
not always succeeded to get everything we set out to do. Issues remain
unresolved, such as council housing; a new graveyard; public toilets;
Goleen water and sewage; Schull water; Goleen, Barleycove and
Ballyrisode carparking, and many more, but our achievements far
outweigh anything we couldn't get done, and with the completion of
our community centre around the corner, and many more projects in
Crookhaven, Goleen, Toormore, Dunbeacon and Lowertown in the
pipeline, there are exciting times ahead for the Goleen and District
Community Council.

GOLEEN CREAMERY

by Denis Downey

Until the mid-1940s the western two thirds of the parish separated their own milk at home, made butter from the cream and sold it to the local shops. In 1946 'West Cork Dairy Disposal', based at Aughadown, started a separating service which was known at the time as the travelling creamery. It contained a large separator and weighing facilities inside this large covered-over lorry and was operated by two employees.

The lorry driver operated the separator and gave out the skim milk while the other employee, who was a creamery manager, weighed the milk, took butter fat samples and recorded all details of quality and the amount of skim milk to be given back to each farmer after separating.

The travelling creamery to Goleen had three locations for separating, one, which was the first each morning, at Lissigriffin where the road branches to Kilmoe graveyard, the next stop was at Ballydevlin, at the first cross to the right, a quarter of a mile past Goleen village, and the third separation took place at the crossroads a few hundred yards from Dunmanus Castle.

In 1959 a site was purchased and a new creamery and stores were built in the townland of Knockeenageragh, 1 mile to the west of Goleen village, which was midway between the Lissigriffin and Ballydevlin separating platforms. The site was purchased from the late Florence O'Driscoll and the building contractor was Michael Holland from Castlehaven. When it opened, the milk from Dunmanus area was brought to Goleen creamery by lorry. It opened on the 20th June 1959, having a milk supply from 180 farmers.

The first manager was Diarmuid O'Sullivan and Maurice McCarthy was the engine driver, who held that job until separating stopped in 1988. The first store manager was the late Michael O'Connor followed by Jimmy Downey and then Anthony O'Callaghan, who still has that position but sadly on a three-day week since 2006. Diarmuid

O'Sullivan left Goleen creamery in 1964 and was replaced by John Hickey, who remained there until separating ceased in 1988.

In 1975 all dairy disposal branches were taken over by Drinagh Co-Op, but sadly the greater part of them are now closed. In 1959 when the creamery opened it had 180 suppliers; today there are only 22 farmers producing milk in that area. About five farmers' milk is collected at the creamery, the other seventeen being collected at their farmyards. The first representative from the Goleen branch on the committee of management was the late Eugene Downing, followed by Diarmuid Cullinane, Gerard O'Donovan and at present Richard O'Connell.

That is the history of our creamery and the great changes in milk production and management from the early days when all cows were milked by hand, and the milk taken to the creamery in churns by donkey and cart, or horse and cart, every morning, where all the farmers met and had plenty time to talk and discuss all the local happenings.

On Monday mornings the bowling score was discussed, he who played the 'sop' every time and won the score by a bowl of odds, to the accurate corner forward on the football team, who put two points over the bar from out near the side-line, and the full forward who missed the 14-yard free from in front of the posts, the one his mother would have scored with her eyes closed. No Monday morning conversation would be complete without a discussion on the 'Long Dance' the previous night, who saw such-and-such a girl being brought home on the crossbar of some Raleigh bicycle, or the still-luckier girl who was escorted home on the pillion seat of someone and a quarter horsepower Bantam motorbike. These were the happier 1950s and 1960s. Twenty to thirty years ago, any town or city children visiting a farm were always anxious to see cows being milked, today 80–90% of the local farmers' children never have seen a cow being milked, so is that what we call progress and the Celtic Tiger? If your answer is yes, maybe the following poem will help you to remember our past.

The farmhouse I used to know,
Is now a fading dream,
The cows I milked each morn
And night, and seldom got the cream.
The horses tackled to the plough
From daylight unto dark,
And the early morning call I got
To be up before the lark.

There was no television then,
And we led more healthy lives,
And husbands went to dances
With their well contented wives.
The children had good manners
Always saying Sir and Mam,
and considered themselves lucky
If they could get bread and jam.

The farmer was complaining
As he will always do,
And you got a sack of 'praities'
For about a bob or two.
A penny in your pocket
Would make you feel a king,
And strikes, I can assure you,
Never heard such a thing.

The farmhouse has changed a lot,
There's a fridge inside the door,
The motor car replaced the horse,
That old house is used no more.
A machine replaced the human hands
To milk the same old cows,
And the days we had at harvest time
You cannot find them now.

Now, am I missing something
For the fact I'm growing old?
Or are the people happier
As we now are often told?
The stories by the fireside
I fear we will hear no more,
My wish is to be back again
In those happy days of yore.

The above photo was taken on the morning of the official opening of Goleen creamery on 20th June 1959. Included are Fr MacSweeney, who performed the blessing, Michael Holland, building contractor, PJ Kerrisk, general manager, 'Dairy Disposal' Aughadown, Diarmuid O'Sullivan, branch manager, Maurice McCarthy, engine driver. The only farmer in the photo who supplied milk on that morning, is on the right-hand side, front row. He decided some time later that there must surely be an easier way, so he headed for Leinster House and will still be going there for another five years at least, his name is Paddy Sheehan, TD.

ROMAN CATHOLIC CHURCHES AND CLERGY IN THE PARISH OF GOLEEN

by *Michael McCarthy*

Writing in the diocesan magazine *The Fold* in the 1970s, the late Very Rev Jim Coombes, parish priest, Timoleague, states that the few scanty details of RC priests and churches comes from the 1704 register of the Church of Ireland Bishop Dive Downes and a further report in 1731.

The report states that Teige Coughlan, aged about fifty, was priest of Kilmoe and part of Schull and lived on Long Island The Bishop of Ossary in Kilkenny ordained him. In 1731 Rev Paul Limerick, rector of Schull and Kilmoe, reported that John Hinnegan, PP, had Teige Callanane as his assistant. They had two thatched mass-houses in which mass was celebrated – one in Schull and one in Kilmoe.

Paul Limerick noted that a number of priests were landing at Crookhaven Harbour from France and other countries, mostly friars, and travelling inland. The history of the four churches in the townland of Arderrawinny in the parish of Goleen is contained in a well-researched article written in the *Mizen Journal* in 1996 by the late Michael R O'Donovan. The following is only a short history taken from the full report.

The earliest church recorded in Arderrawinny was a thatched mass-house in the south end of the townland. It dated from about 1733–1800. No trace of this church now exists. It was replaced by a thatched structure some hundred yards to the Southeast. The church was built before 1805; Rev Florence Crowley at a yearly rent of £1-2s-9d secured the lease of the site from Jer McCarthy.

On Sunday, 17th April 1825, the thatched roof fell in during the celebration of mass and several of the congregation were injured. Throughout the year of 1825, worship continued in the open.

Ballinskea Church, which stood on the hillside at Arderrawinny, was built by Fr Michael Prior, PP, Kilmoe, Goleen, who was a native of County Tipperary. This church served the faithful for 140 years. Richard Hull presented the site; he also donated 20 guineas towards the building. Hull performed the ceremony of laying the foundation stone in June 1826. He also permitted the quarrying of stone and lifting of bog timber from his Leamcon land. His son and heir contributed £3 to the building costs.

Rev Traill, rector of Schull, subscribed 30 guineas. The church, dedicated to St Patrick, was in use towards the end of 1826. An inscription stone was inserted in the front wall of the church; it was indicative of the bright period of ecumenical spirit that prevailed at the time. The inscription read: 'To the glory of God this chapel was erected by Protestants and Roman Catholics, founded AD 1826 jubilee'.

This inscription is the only enduring relic of this church to survive. It was rescued from the demolition of the church in 1975 by the late Michael R O'Donovan and, in the 1990s, Fr Denis Cashman had it placed on the inside wall of the Church of the Seven Sacraments. The church at Ballinskea was demolished in 1975 by diocesan decree. Demolition contractors were Messrs O'Mahony & Barry. For a period after construction the parish priest lived in a house nearby. This house was later used as a dispensary after the priests moved to a house in Ballydevlin, Goleen. Fr Jerome Kiely, CC, celebrated the last mass at Ballinskea on Sunday, 3rd December 1967.

A new church for Goleen Parish

The following is a copy from a letter issued by Rev James Horgan, PP, and Rev Michael Dineen, CC, in 1965:

> Dear Friend,
> Goleen Parish needs a new church at Ballinskea. The old church is now that it would need very extensive repairs to make it safe for use. It has been decided by his Lordship the Bishop of Cork and Ross that the most practical, and in the long run the most economical, plan to adopt is to abandon the old church and erect a new structure at Arderrawinny.
>
> The cost of this proposed scheme is £35,000 to £40,000 to which the central fund will contribute £10,000. We know that the people of Goleen will strain their resources to make this plan a reality. We also know that it would be impossible to expect the present

population of Goleen parish to subscribe even half this
sum, however good their intentions, however prodigal
their generosity.

Most reluctantly we must appeal to those who have
left Goleen district but who still have ties of blood and
kinship and friendship to lend a helping hand. Motive,
which inspires this undertaking, is the dictate that Our
Lord should have a decent church and home among his
people. Please help us to give Him that church and home.

Subscriptions to be sent to V Rev James Horgan, PP,
and Michael Dineen, CC, Goleen, Co Cork.

Copies of this letter were sent by parishioners to relatives in the USA
and England. There was a big response to the appeal. At home money
was raised through collections, bazaars, concerts and dances. As in
the building of the old church, the ecumenical spirit was again alive
and well in the parish.

Fr Horgan, in one of his reports of the success of the fundraising,
publicly paid tribute to Canon GC Hillard, rector of Goleen and The
Alter, and his parishioners for their generosity. The foundation stone
of the new church on a site on the main Schull–Goleen road was laid
on 26th April 1966 by Most Rev Cornelius Lucey and Fr James
Horgan. The late Michael Collins gave this site free.

The contractors were O'Driscoll & Hourihane of Bantry. Work was
completed in record time and the subscriptions were so great that the
cost of the church was paid for before completion. Named 'The
Church of the Seven Sacraments' it was consecrated on 8th December
1967 by the Most Rev Dr Lucey.

The church was crowded for the occasion and Fr Jerome Kiely, CC,
delivered the homily. The first person to be baptised in the new
church was Michael Collins, nephew of Michael who donated the site.

Goleen churches

The Griffith Valuation reports of 1852 refer to the church and buildings
in the townland of Boulysallagh. This was the site that later became the
priest's residence. The church on this site served the parishioners from
1806–1854. A plaque on the wall beside the main altar of Kilmurry
parish church in Cloughdubh has the following inscription:

'To the memory of Rev John Canon Foley, pastor of
Kilmurry, for a period of 26 years. In trying years that

followed the famine as parish priest of West Schull his energies were daily taxed in attending the material as well as the spiritual interests of his flock. As his solicitude for the beauty of God's House this church as well as the churches at Canovee and Goleen are an enduring monument. He died on 30th June 1893.'

According to records he was parish priest at Goleen 1848–1855. According to Griffith, work was in progress in the new parish church in 1852. Richard Notter, landlord, gave the site, for the sum of one shilling. His brother, who was an architect and lived at Lisacahha House, designed the roof. The stone for the building came from Crookhaven and Mallavogue. Timber used in the church was wreck timber recovered from the sea along the coast. The roof and ceiling were cut by Daniel O'Sullivan from Ballydehob, who lived in High Street, Goleen. Families bought seats for £1 each for their own needs on both side aisles. The people of Crookhaven bought seats in the south aisle (left side of the altar). And the people of Goleen bought the seats in the north aisle (right side of the altar). In later years people referred to the aisles as the Crookhaven and Goleen aisles.

Jim O'Sullivan, a carpenter of Colleras, made a number of the church seats. On 11th October 1854 Most Rev William Delaney, Bishop of Cork, blessed and dedicated the new parish church at Goleen, giving it the title 'Our Lady Star of the Sea and St Patrick'.

On the centenary in 1954 major work was carried out under the guidance of Fr John O'Mahony, PP, and Curate Fr Con Lucey. The main source of funding came from card drives and dances. All the plaster was removed from the inside walls because of dampness. The walls were battened and plaster bounded. The main floors of the church were flagged stones; these were removed and replaced with tiles. The new sacristy and side room were built. The altar was moved and the spire raised to its present height. The work was undertaken by contractors O'Sullivan Brothers, Seaview, Bantry. Two local men, Michael Barry and Michael Sweeney were employed during the work.

In September 2004 work took place on the 150th anniversary of the church. The church was painted, new carpet was fitted in the sanctuary, and flood lighting was installed. On Friday 8th October Most Rev Dr J Buckley concelebrated mass assisted by Fr Hugh McLoughlin, SMA, CC, and Fr Bernard O'Donovan, PP Schull and Adm. Goleen. Former parish priest Fr John Cotter, PP Monkstown, delivered the homily.

The longest-serving parish priest in Goleen was Fr Timothy O'Sullivan from 1917–1939. The longest-serving curate in the parish was Fr Jerome Kiely, who was CC from 1967–1983. Five parish priests died whilst ministering in Goleen and are buried in the adjacent churchyard: V Rev Daniel O'Connell, PP, died 17th October 1897; V Rev John Hurley, PP, died 1st September 1946; V Rev John O'Mahony died 26th July 1957; V Rev John Hegarty, PP, died 7th September 1970; V Rev Denis Barry, PP, died 25th December 1971.

Two of Goleen's curates died whilst attached to the parish. A headstone at a grave in Toames churchyard in Kilmichael parish reads: 'In memory of Rev Timothy O'Mahony died on 12th September 1888 in his 30th year and the 4th of his ministry'.

Fr O'Mahoney came to Goleen in 1886. Whilst visiting a parishioner he contracted typhoid fever. He died in the presbytery six days later. With him when he died was Mr Barth Wooll, a schoolteacher in Goleen. Fr O'Mahoney was taken back to Toames for burial. He was an uncle of Fr John O'Mahoney who died in 1957.

In Dunmanway churchyard a memorial reads: 'In memory of Rev John Bernard, CC, Watergrasshill, died 10th February 1917 aged 29 yrs'.

From this information it will appear that Fr Bernard was transferred from Watergrasshill to Goleen. Regulations at the time were that priests were notified of transfers during the week and were to minister in their new parishes on the next Sunday. Fr Bernard had done weekly duties in Goleen and on his journey back became ill and died. His family arranged his burial in Dunmanway.

The records of the diocese state that Rev John Daly, CC, appointed to Goleen in 1864 came from Cork city and it involved two days' travelling.

Priests of Goleen parish since 1817

1817   Fr Michael Prior, PP (interred at Ballinora Churchyard)
1826   Fr Florence O'Crowley, CC
1828   Fr Laurence O'Sullivan, PP (interred at Ballygarvan Churchyard)
1828   Fr Michael Begley, CC (lived in Crookhaven)
1837   Fr Thomas Staunton, CC
1839   Fr Denis O'Donoghue, CC
1843   Fr John Hurley, CC
1844   Fr T Barrett, CC
1847   Fr Charles McCarthy, CC
1848   Fr John Foley, PP (interred at Kilmurry)
1848   Fr Thomas Nyhan, CC
1851   Fr Charles O'Connell, CC

1853 Fr Cornelius Twomey, CC
1855 Fr Thomas Walsh, PP
1855 Fr William Murphy, CC (interred at Farnivane Churchyard)
1857 Fr Timothy Murray, CC (interred at Douglas Churchyard)
1859 Fr Denis Forrest, CC (later served as PP)
1863 Fr Timothy Holland, PP (interred at Innishannon
       Churchyard)
1863 Fr John Lyons, CC (interred at Kinsale Churchyard)
1864 Fr John Daly, CC (interred at St Joseph's Cemetery, Cork)
1865 Fr David O'Mahoney, CC (interred at St Joseph's Cemetery,
       Cork)
1865 Fr Patrick Hurley, CC
1867 Fr Cornelius O'Keeffe, PP
1867 Fr Cornelius O'Sullivan, CC (interred at Enniskeane
       Churchyard)
1869 Fr Patrick O'Connell, CC (interred at Ovens Churchyard)
1870 Fr Patrick O'Neill, CC (interred at Minane Bridge Churchyard)
1873 Fr D O'Sullivan, CC
1873 Fr Daniel O'Connell (interred at Goleen Churchyard)
1875 Fr Denis Bernard, CC (interred at Newcestown Churchyard)
1879 Fr Patrick Dineen, CC
1881 Fr Con O'Leary, CC (interred at Inchigeela Churchyard)
1886 Fr Timothy O'Mahony, CC (interred at Toames Churchyard)
1888 Fr Jeremiah J Crowley, CC
1892 Fr Denis Cummins CC (interred at Bandon Churchyard)
1896 Fr Michael Cotter, CC (interred at Newcestown Churchyard)
1897 Fr Denis Forrest, PP (interred at Drimoleague Churchyard)
1898 Fr John O'Callaghan, PP
1899 Fr JJ Ahern, CC (interred at St Joseph's Cemetery, Cork)
1901 Fr James O'Sullivan, CC
1905 Fr John V Hurley, CC (later served as PP)
1906 Fr Michael O'Leary, CC (interred at Schull Churchyard)
1909 Fr Patrick A Desmond, PP (interred at Innishannon
       Churchyard)
1910 Fr Patrick Daly, CC (interred at Schull Churchyard)
1912 Fr John McCarthy, CC (interred at Ballinspittle Churchyard)
1917 Fr Timothy of Sullivan, PP (interred at Bantry Churchyard)
1917 Fr John Bernard, CC (interred at Dunmanway Churchyard)
1917 Fr JJ Coakley, CC (interred at Dunmanway Churchyard)
1922 Fr CM Creed, CC (interred at Lota Cemetery, Glanmire)
1923 Fr Daniel J McCarthy, CC (interred at St Finbarr's Cemetery,
       Cork)

1929 Fr Jerome O'Riordan, CC (interred at Minane Bridge Churchyard)

1933 Fr Charles O'Riordan, CC (interred at St Finbarr's Cemetery, Cork)

1936 Fr James Cummins, CC (later served as PP)

1939 Fr John Hurley, PP (interred at Goleen Churchyard)

1939 Fr John McSweeney, CC (interred at Cloughdubh Churchyard)

1942 Fr Charles O'Connor, CC (interred at St Finbarr's Cemetery, Cork)

1945 Fr Michael Lucey, CC (interred at Innishannon Churchyard)

1946 Fr John O'Mahoney, PP (interred at Goleen Churchyard)

1951 Fr Cornelius Lucey, CC (interred at St Colman's Cemetery, Macroom)

1955 Fr Denis O'Donoghue, CC (interred at Crosshaven Churchyard)

1957 Fr Florence McSweeney, PP (interred at Goggins Hill Churchyard)

1958 Fr Wm F Murphy, CC (later served as PP)

1962 Fr Timothy A Coffey PP (interred at St Bridget's Cemetery, Crosshaven)

1962 Fr Liam O'Mahony, CC

1963 Fr James Cummins, PP (interred at Turner's Cross Churchyard, Cork)

1964 Fr Michael Dineen, CC (interred at Glounthane Churchyard)

1964 Fr James Horgan, PP (interred at Ballinlough Churchyard)

1967 Fr Jerome Kiely, CC

1969 Fr John Hegarty, PP (interred at Goleen Churchyard)

1971 Fr Denis Barry, PP (interred at Goleen Churchyard)

1973 Fr Michael Kelleher, PP (interred at Cloughdubh Churchyard)

1976 Fr Diarmuid O'Connor, PP (interred at Farnivane Churchyard)

1982 Fr Wm F Murphy, PP (interred at North Kilmurry, NW Cork)

1987 Fr Sean Buckley, PP (interred at St Elfin's, Kinsale)

1991 Fr John Cotter, PP

1995 Fr Denis Cashman, PP (last resident PP)

1999 Fr Michael Nolan, Adm

1999 Fr Hugh McLoughlin, SMA, CC

2004 Fr David Hegarty, Adm

2004 Fr Bernard Donovan, Adm

2006 Fr John O'Donovan, CC

Acknowledgements

Margaret O'Donovan and family, Leamcon; Mizen Historical Society for permission to use extracts from *Mizen Journal* 1996; Fr Frank Buckley, Diocesan Office, Cork; Karen O'Sullivan, Civil Registration, Skibbereen; Mary A Downey, Goleen.

Dear Old West Cork in the Parish of Kilmoe

Dear old West Cork, Lisagriffin townland
The place I was born, down by the White Strand,
Which is bound by Ballyvogue, Dough and Canawee
Is the prettiest spot you ever could see.

The tide, it runs in twice every day,
Over the White Strand to Barleycove Bay.
There is Clohane and Corran, Cahir and Stuckeen,
Dunlough, Carrigmanus, Gurtbrack and Balteen,
and the foaming Atlantic, Mizen Head and the Brow
Where many a proud ship has broken her bow.

And next comes the Fastnet and yonder Cape Clear,
With Goleen, Crookhaven and Rock Island so near.
Now climb up the hill to Knockamadrai
And there see Dunmanus and the holy ground by the sea.
So romantic a paradise you never did view,
As dear old West Cork in the parish of Kilmoe.

To the west is Dunkelly, Gurduv and Lackavan,
All over her coast grow seaweed and mivawn.
There is Dhuroad and Bird Island, Carrigicat and Cloughanekilleen,
Go up to Fadah and look down at Mileen...

I can never forget Lisagriffin's old school,
Master O'Leary and his famous rod and rule.
We played in the strand around the old swimming hole,
Where the air, it has life and pure was the soul.

The people who lived there went down to their clay,
In honour and happiness, there by the bay.
With my heart and my soul, I now bid thee adieu,
Dear old West Cork in the parish of Kilmoe.

Barley Cove

Some wise old heads thinking of how they would beat the bookies at Goleen Horse Races.

SOUTH WEST CORK CHURCH OF IRELAND

by Betty Barry

The Mizen peninsula has seen many changes. In olden days, the people worked hard. Today, every walk of life is different. People travel all over the world on holiday and Ireland has become a tourist place where many people come and enjoy their time here; they return again. In Kilmoe, we have Mizen Visitors' Centre, Barleycove Hotel, a caravan site and plenty of accommodation locally.

In Goleen village there is a beautiful Roman Catholic Church, dedicated 1852. There is also a Church of Ireland church at Crookhaven village. During 1699 Bishop D Downes of Cork visited Kilmoe parish and saw ruins of a 'Chapel of Ease', which was dedicated to St Mullagha at the entrance to Crookhaven. Dr Peter Browne, DD of Dublin, was later appointed to Cork diocese. During that time, he came on a visit to Schull and Kilmoe and, found the Chapel of Ease in ruins. Dr Browne got it rebuilt during 1717, at his own expense, and it's known today as St Brendan's Church. Services were taken in that church on Sundays and feast days for the parish, and those who came in boats to the harbour. At the present time, ecumenical services are held there during July and August, taken by Rev E Lynch, Rector of Kilmoe Union.

In the cemetery surrounding the church there are lots of graves. One is of Isaac N Nottor, who died at 67 years. The Nottors came from Herrengberg, Germany, in 1631. They were landlords and architects. They gave the ground free to the protestants (Church of Ireland) of Kilmoe to build the church on, and also contributed to the building of it in 1841. It was also funded by ecclesiastical commissions, who gave £582 and private donations £150. The final service was 30th June 1991.

In the church, the stained-glass window in the sanctuary was dedicated in memory of Dr James McCormick, MD of Kilmoe, and the Rev WA Fisher, rector, who both served faithfully in West Cork during the Famine years. The end window is in memory of Mrs McCormick, wife of Dr McCormick, who died in 1884. The Holy Table was presented by Mrs K Wilson and her sister Mrs E Massey in memory of their grandfather Rev Thomas O'Grady, who was curate of the parish, 1831–1839. Also of their parents, Canon WW O'Grady and Mrs M O'Grady, Bantry. The organ was also presented in memory of Rev WA Fisher. The lecton was in memory of Mrs White, Goleen, presented by her family. The baptismal font was given by the family of Mrs Roe, 1878. The sanctuary was redecorated in memory of Michael Burchill, Lackanakea.

'To the Glory of God', 'By his wife and family' – there are more plaques on the walls in memory of Notters, Wilkinsons, Burchills and Roycrofts. In that graveyard are the graves of three rectors: the Rev JJ Stoney, died May 1900, age 59; the Rev RH Carroll, who was accidentally drowned on his way to visit a sick parishioner, near Crookhaven, 1911; and Rev AA Wilson, who died December 1965, age 83. There was another church on a little land belonging to Mr Hungerford in Ballyrisode. It had been built by Rev JJ Stoney, who died before it was completed. The church was dedicated in his memory as 'The Stoney Memorial Church'.

Altar Church (*Téampail na mboic*) was built during the Famine years and was paid for by the payments the Rev Fisher received for the poor. He employed the people and got the church completed and gave them work instead of handing the funds out. Rev Fisher got the fever a second time and died 7th August 1880. He is buried in Dublin.

1900	Rev CGW Brew	
1927	Rev AA Wilson	
1962	Rev RCB Hilliard	Died December 1965
1978	Rev LA Elliott	
1983	Rev NM Cummins	

Rectors of Altar

1842	Rev WA Fisher
1880	Rev EH Hopley
	Rev AH Carroll
	Rev RH Hadden
	Rev JU Atken
	Rev JA Connolly
	Rev RJ Colthrust
	Rev CR Chevasse
	Rev MT Lord
	Rev CB Roberts

Rev FJ Powell
Rev AA Quelch
Rev C Hilliard
Rev E Robinson
Canon LA Elliott
Canon NM Cummins
Canon HM Wakeman
Rev E Lynch, Rector of Kilmoe Union

Schools

Three Castle Head, opened 1845
Rock Island, opened, 1845
Ballydevlin, opened 1845

Entering Crookhaven on route to Crook Road Races.

BROW HEAD GRANITE QUARRY

by Jim O'Meara

Introduction

When the people of this parish travel along the harbour road opposite Crookhaven, or, when they look across the harbour from the village, they hardly notice the row of dark sheds by the roadside, the battered, crumbling pier, the grey concrete walls of the giant stone bins, or the scarred expanse of hillside slowly being healed by time. We have lived with 'The Quarry' for more than 70 years and we take it all for granted. It is only seafarers – entering the splendid harbour for the first time – and first-time passers by on the road that are puzzled, intrigued and possibly shocked by it. It is hard for us now to imagine that it was a place of dust, noise, industry, shouting and laughter for more than ten years, until the beginning of World War II in early September 1939, and that – during the 'hungry thirties' – it provided employment for up to 70 local people at peak times. For 30 more years the plant and machinery were kept in working order until 1969, when the scrap merchants were sent in and the place was reduced to the gaunt, rusting skeleton, which it is today.

First impressions

When I first explored the Quarry, as a schoolboy, in the early fifties, it was a fascinating place to visit. In the tarred sheds by the roadside the generators and other mysterious engines stood. They were painted green, with gleaming brass work, as you see in science museums today. Up on the hillside the giant Crosley diesel engine crouched in its shed – ready to drive the pitiless jaws of the crushers when required. Out in the open, on the cut-back rock plateau at the cliff face, was a complete miniature railway, with branching tracks, points and black stone trucks lined up ready to roll.

Most fascinating of all was the Quarry office, a time capsule from the 1930s, with its desks, chairs, typewriters and files. The calendar for 1939 hung on the wall showing the month of September. A sheaf of telegrams, impaled on a spike, gave information on the passage of ships to and from Crookhaven. Every thing was in perfect order, waiting for the next day to begin, but that day never came.

Beginnings

How and why did the whole enterprise begin? About 80 years have passed since that time and information is hard to come by. Sadly, most of the people who worked there, or even those who saw it in operation, have now passed away, but the few who remain have valuable stories to tell. In addition, there are a few dusty files and ledgers from the Quarry's operating life and some newspapers from the period. The earliest record I have seen is a diary from 1927, which appears to be an official log of work being carried out. The opening entry is for 1st March, reporting work on the completion of a bungalow for the project. Over the year the scale and extent of the operation and the workforce increased. Work commenced on the engine house and the pier and the whole infrastructure began to be put in place.

An article written by Florence O'Connor for *The Southern Star*, 4th January 1930, reports the Quarry as just commencing full operations after three years of construction work, costing more than £30,000 sterling. He points out that the company name: 'Brow Head Granite Quarry', was misleading, as no granite occurs in this area. He describes the local rock as a mixture of quartz and sandstone, extremely hard and very suitable as a road surfacing material.

By the twenties and thirties of the last century, the age of the motorcar had arrived and the roads in the south-east of England, as they were everywhere else, were being rapidly improved to make life easier for the motorist. The problem, he writes, was that in the area of England, south of the Thames, the local, chalky rock was too soft for road making, so alternative sources had to be found. The steep cliffs on the north shore of Crookhaven Harbour were ideal for the purpose.

How then was the stone to be transported? Well, at that time, much coal was being shipped to Irish ports from the coalfields of Britain by fleets of small colliers, which were returning empty. Coal boats bound home from south and west coast Irish ports were chartered to load cargoes of stone in Crookhaven and, although freight rates were low, it was worth their while to do so. Jerry O'Mahony of Crookhaven has told me that he remembers seeing as many as three small coasters at a time anchored in the harbour, waiting their turn to load crushed stone at the Quarry Pier. Since the harbour at that point is quite shallow, the laden boats departing had little water to spare and John O'Driscoll of Goleen – who is one of the last survivors of those who worked at the Quarry – described to me how their propellers churned up a muddy wake behind them as they steamed away.

How the work was done

How was the stone processed for shipment? To start with, holes were drilled in the rock face, gelignite sticks were inserted, tamped down with sand and detonated. Jerry O'Mahony reports that blasting usually took place around midday and again at 5 p.m. The harbour road would be closed, the warning sounded and the hillside would erupt in a booming crescendo of noise, smoke and dust. The north side of the harbour would be churned up by a hail of falling stones. Then the air would clear, the frightened sea birds would settle again and relative peace would be restored.

The newly dislodged boulders would then be battered with massive 28-pound hammers by quarrymen to produce rocks capable of being lifted into the trucks by the strong men who worked there. The trucks would then be pushed by hand across a weigh bridge and down to the steel jaws of the two (later three) stone crushers which, between them, were capable of crushing 35 tons of stone per hour. The crushed stone would then be screened, sorted and directed into the giant holding bins above the road. In this part of the operation, gravity was the main source of power as the stone cascaded into the bins.

Shipping

Through the thirties there are numerous references in the files of *The Southern Star* to shipping movements to and from the Quarry. For example, on Saturday, 13th November 1937, the *Star* reported that the SS *President*, the SS *Kyle of Bute*, the SS *Brookston* and the MV *Westerschelde* sailed during the week with more than 3,000 tons of stone for London and Ipswich. Again, on Saturday, 30th July 1938, the SS *Stanley Force* and the SS *Murville* sailed for the same ports with 1,450 tons. On 7th December 1938, the SS *Parknasilla* was reported as arriving from Fenit to load 1,050 tons of stone and stone dust for London.

The availability of ships limited the work at the Quarry and at times the bins filled up with stone; crushing therefore had to stop, resulting in the layoff of workers. These periods of layoff became more frequent in later years, according to John O'Driscoll and, with the onset of war in September 1939, when the coal trade to Ireland ended at once, the work at the Quarry also ceased. Jack O'Sullivan of Arduslough, remembers the fateful day well – seeing his father, Denis, and his neighbour, Paddy McCarthy, returning up the hillside with the news that their jobs were no more. The grief and gloom in those two households was experienced in many houses in the parish on that day.

Working conditions

What were conditions like for the workforce? According to Florence O'Connor, whose 1930 article I've already drawn on, the pay and conditions were better than those offered by Cork County Council at that time. The wages offered seem pitifully small by today's inflated standards, but were considered good at that time. The wages paid to a labourer were nine old pence per hour, or less than five and a half cents per hour in our money! This rate is recorded in the wage ledgers I have seen. It is true that charge hands, fitters, drillers and blacksmiths were paid at a higher rate and received the equivalent of eight cents an hour – almost. I have been told that there was an additional piecework rate of nine pence per ton of stone moved, but the ledgers make no reference to this and it is hard to see how it could be applied to those not working at the stone face. However, it might explain the long hours worked by some men. A six-day week was worked, with some Sunday working, mainly by fitters, presumably for maintenance.

The hours worked were very long and there was no extra rate for overtime. Fifty to 60 hours per week were commonly worked – although above 70 was quite common. Richard Hurley, a labourer, is credited with a massive 89 hours on the week ending 18th June 1930 – although this may have included piecework. For this he was paid a not-so-massive three pounds five shillings and nine pence, or about four euro and seventy cents. However, the 'world record' may be held by Alex McFarlane, a fitter, who is credited with 102 hours on the same week, including twelve and a half hours Sunday working – with 18 hours on two of the days! For all this he got four pounds fifteen shillings and eleven pence, or about six euro and eighty cents. However, a more usual figure for a week's wages would be a little more than two pounds, or about three euro. Company files record the weekly amounts sent to the Provincial Bank of Ireland in Schull (which was where the library now is), to cover the weekly wage bill for all employees and, while the amounts varied quite a lot, depending on the amount of work going on, a cheque for one hundred and forty pounds (about two hundred euro) would make it a good week.

Working conditions were very hard, the work was very heavy. Who would now want to swing an enormous 28-pound hammer six days a week? Jack O'Sullivan still has one of those awesome implements, which I have handled myself and could do little more than lift! He reports seeing old hammers that were worn almost to the boss from hard usage. He says that the boots they wore, which were heavy duty and cost them the equivalent of about 43 cents, wore out after a few weeks – so much was the wear and tear!

Conditions were noisy, dusty and dangerous. There were no ear-muffs or breathing masks and the injuries ledger I've seen lists many severe cuts, bruises and fractures. Falling rocks and hammers caused many injuries. One man had an anvil fall on his foot and at least two were injured by runaway stone trucks. A more serious accident occurred when a premature rock face explosion caught Tom Thessings of Leenane and an explosives supervisor named Gordon. They were quite badly injured but, fortunately, escaped the full force of the blast, which would certainly have killed them. One tragic acci-dent occurred when Jack Thessings (Tom's brother), a fitter at the plant, was hit on the head by a moving part of a crusher. His skull was fractured and the injury resulted in his death.

Conclusion

The memory of all these events is fast fading away and the Quarry is no more than an archaeological site, destined to crumble away with the passage of time. It remains the property of the successors of the original company, who were Rowe Bros of Liverpool. So, what should happen to it now? Should the old sheds be cleared away to enhance the beauty of the harbour? What could be done to soften the harsh ugliness of the bins? I lament the scrapping carried out in 1969; it was a shame to saw up those beautiful engines, which had been kept in pristine condition by Jim Maguire, Paddy Hourihane, Jack O'Sullivan and John O'Driscoll over the years and which were perhaps the only examples of their type left in working order at the time. Today we could have had a working museum of the quarrying industry of the first half of the last century, which would perhaps have been a fitting memorial to all of those who toiled there.

MIZEN HEAD SIGNAL STATION VISITOR CENTRE – THE IRISH LIGHTS MIZEN HEAD FOG SIGNAL STATION

by Sue Hill

Introduction and background

Mizen Head, the most southwesterly point of Ireland, spelt danger to ships for centuries until the Irish Lights Signal Station was built there in 1908. In 1993 Mizen Tourism Co-operative Society Ltd was established to seize the initiative to develop a unique attraction at the station as the last keepers left the Mizen Head Signal Station made redundant by automation. Together with the Fastnet Rock Lighthouse, the Signal Station has been involved with the advances in technology for safety at sea from the explosive fog signal through the first radio beacon in Ireland to the present day DGPS grid. The new visitor centre was called 'Mizen Vision! The Irish Lights Signal Station Visitor Centre' and it had in excess of 217,000 visitors in the first five years with 52,000 in 1998. In the years 1998–July 2003 a further 205,000 visitors paid to go down to the Signal Station across the Bridge. In 2001 a new facilities and interpretive building was opened above near the car park. The Mizen Head Visitor Centre site is in three locations. The 'Visitor Centre Above' at the car park, the 'Path On the Way' down to the 'Signal Station Below'. There is a ten-minute walk between the buildings down a steep path and across the Bridge.

Project Phase 1 (completed)

In the first phase of Mizen Vision! the Signal Station was opened to the public for the first time in June 1994 with displays and exhibits in the former keepers' quarters about the lives of the keepers, Mizen wildlife, wrecks and the story of the Fastnet Lighthouse. In 1996 Mizen Vision! won a Ford Ireland Environmental Award. It was short-listed twice for a AIB Better Ireland Award, winning the National Prize for Small Rural Business in 1999. It was awarded Fuchsia Brand status by West Cork Leader Co-operative in 1998. This development created an integrated, all-weather, authentic, visitor experience. It has added significantly to the experience of a visit to the Visitor Centre.

Mizen Café and Shop@ the Mizen, toilets, Navigational Aids Simulator, Automatic Weather Station, displays and interpretation have given comfort and interest to the visitor. The concept of the displays in the new building is to explain the use of modern technology in safety at sea. The modern way of collecting weather data, unlike the manual methods used by the lightkeepers, is with a computerised automatic weather station (AWS). Mizen Tourism purchased a system from Mason Technology.

There is much more to Mizen Head Visitor Centre. The location at Ireland's most southwesterly point is dramatic, with the 99 Steps and a spectacular Arched Bridge. In the former keepers' quarters there are displays about the life of the keepers and the environment of the Mizen. The new building has artwork by Jules Thomas, who has created a stunning mural showing the Mizen landscape looking back from the Fastnet Rock Lighthouse. The 1/10th model of the lighthouse has been made by Geoff McCarthy and Dave Otway. In the entrance Sheena Wood and Kurt Lyndorff of the Ewe Art Centre, Glengarriff (formerly of Goleen), created three sculptures: 'Water on Rock', a water feature, 'Sky to Seabed', a tile mural and 'Lighthouse Crafts', five pairs of hands showing lighthouse keepers' crafts.

In Mizen Café John Eagle's photographs of the lighthouses from Old Head of Kinsale to Cromwell Point, Valentia, dominate the wall alongside Richard Mills' exquisite photos of local wildlife, flowers and ancient monuments. On the gable is a mural by Russell Barrett of the Bridge and the Signal Station across the other side. There are a café, shop and toilets to give comfort to the visitor. The development has given an experience to people who for various reasons do not walk down to the Signal Station.

Mizen Vision! was renamed Mizen Head Signal Station Visitor Centre on the opening of the new building in 2001. In 2003 Mizen Head Signal Station was included in the *Reader's Digest/Sunday Times* 100 Most Amazing Places in Britain and Ireland.

Project Phase 2

This phase of the project develops the 'learn to' aspects of the project in five interrelated themes: safety at sea, communications, weather,

tides and currents, and geology, There are two strands to these activities with Visitors and Schools Programmes. These themes are integrated throughout the Visitor Centre site as they follow from the
'Visitor Centre Above', 'Along the Way' to the 'Keepers' Quarters
Below'. Another three rooms have been constructed with more interpretation throughout.

Donation of memorabilia

Commissioners of Irish Lights, Eamonn Doyle, Claire Barrett,
Michael O'Reilly, Arthur O'Sullivan, Ken Austin, the family of the late
Tom Barry, Charles J Haughey, Goleen ICA, Birds Ireland, Birdwatch
Ireland, Irish Whale and Dolphin Group, Donal O'Sullivan, Rosemary
O'Driscoll, Mrs H Glanville, Mrs R Craig-White, Frank Ryan, Peter
Duggan.

Architects: Daly, Barry & Associates. Quantity Surveyor: Jim
Scannell & Associates. Engineers: Diarmuid McCarthy & Associates
Main Contractor: CHOM Ltd. Bank: AIB, Schull and Skibbereen.
Solicitors: Babington, Clarke & Mooney. Accountants:
PriceWaterhouseCoopers and Gordon Lane & Co Development and
Project Management: Sue Hill and Stephen O'Sullivan. Concept
Design: Ed Lamb. Design Advisor: Jules Thomas. Multimedia: Tony
Perrott and Uwe Schiller, UCC, Pat Leonard, Thornhill Bros. Filming:
Ted Dolan and Tish Barry. Navigational Aids Simulator Co-ordina-
tion: Cormac Gebruers, Transas Ltd, Eamonn Doyle, Charternav GPS
Ltd. Automatic Weather Station: Mason Technology. Mizen Tide
Clock: Stokes Clocks, Cork.

The Committee of Management 1994

Dr Brian O'Connell (Chair), William Buckley, Diarmuid Kenneally,
Kathleen Downey, Sue Hill, Michael McCarthy, Maureen Newman,
Dermot Sheehan, Terry Tuite.

The Committee of Management 2000

Dr Brian O'Connell (Chair), William Buckley, Kathleen Downey, Sue
Hill, Michael McCarthy, Maureen Newman, Stephen O'Sullivan,
Dermot Sheehan, John Stuart.

The Committee of Management 2006

Dr Brian O'Connell (Chair), Stephen O'Sullivan, Sue Hill, Maureen
Newman, Dermot Sheehan, William Buckley, Michael McCarthy,
Michael Barnett, Brian Murphy, Reps. Cork County Council.

History of project

March–December 1992

- Lease sought from Commissioners of Irish Lights for Mizen Head Signal Station.
- Application to West Cork LEADER for funding.

December 1992

On receipt of draft lease from CIL and 50% matching funding from LEADER, a public meeting agreed to register a co-operative with the Registry of Friendly Societies.

April 1993

Took over Mizen Head Signal Station and started installing safety fencing.

October 1993

Opened to the public as Mizen Vision! The Irish Lights Signal Station Visitor Centre for the bank holiday weekend to show everyone what was in the Keepers' Quarters before it was changed. One thousand people came through the gates in two days from as far away as Waterford and Limerick.

October 1993–May 1994

Project Phase 1 building and interpretation completed. Matching funds raised by selling shares and sponsorship by Murphy's Brewery and their agent, West Cork Bottling. Car park made by County Council.

Funding

- LEADER grant £30,000
- Matching Funding from Shares (at £25 each) £20,000
- Murphy's Brewery and WCB £19,000
- Own funds from Income £20,000
- Total investment £89,000

June 1994

- Opened the Signal Station to the public. A small portacabin was installed as ticket office, shop and refreshments. There were 32,000 visitors in the first year. As the most southwesterly point of Ireland, the light keepers before automation said there were hundreds of people on the cliffs outside the Bridge every summer.

- Mizen Tourism Co-operative allowed those visitors across the Bridge thereby making business and employment for the area by adding value to an already popular location.

1995

Allied Irish Banks' premises in Goleen were rented by Mizen Tourism Co-operative Society Ltd and opened as a Telecottage/Business Centre. Full office services, information, accommodation reservations and a serviced office for professionals were provided for locals and visitors.

1997

Mizen Tourism bought the building from AIB and continued to provide services until July 2003 when the Telecottage was closed. Since it was opened in 1995 circumstances have changed and most people have computers at home. Mizen Tourism subsidised the tourism information including bureau de change and reservation service, but the Telecottage was not cost effective. It is collateral for the Society for funding and loans.

1996–2001

Project Phase 2, Part 1. The plans were drawn for next phase; funding and planning permission applications were completed. Planning permission was given and funding was in place from:

- West Cork LEADER for construction
- Bord Fáilte/ERDF for interpretation
- Cork County Council and National Millennium Funding for matching funds.

Funding

- Bord Fáilte/ERDF £225,575
- West Cork LEADER £200,000
- Cork County Council £75,000
- National Millennium Funding £70,000
- Own Funds-AIB Term Loan £167,000
- Total £737,575

Work started and finished over a period of 2 years.

March 2001

New building opened (by telephone) by Noel Davern TD, Minister for

Food, at the beginning of the foot and mouth emergency when Mizen Vision! – renamed 'Mizen Head Signal Station' – was closed for six weeks. Final payments from Bord Fáilte/ERDF, West Cork Leader, Cork County Council and National Millennium Funding.

February 2002
Initial application for funding from Bord Fáilte/ERDF in competition for Phase 2 Part 2.

May 2003
Granted permission by Fáilte Ireland to apply for funding.

May 2004
Granted funding by Fáilte Ireland/ERDF 36% €211,428
(Only 2 drawdowns allowed at that stage, which affected construction and interpretive timetable)

June 2004
Granted matching funding by Cork County Council €200,000

December 2005
Granted AIB Term Loan €150,000

April 2005
Mizen Head Signal Station Bridge closed by Commissioners of Irish Lights.

June 2005
Temporary Scaffolding Solution for the Bridge
Constructed and Bridge reopened June 25th €60,000
Funding   Commissioners of Irish Lights €30,000
                    Cork County Council €30,000
                    Inspection fee (Mizen Tourism) . . . . .€400 per month

It was proved at that time that Mizen Head Signal Station Visitor Centre does not have a future without access to the Bridge and the Signal Station.

May 2006
Donation from local well-wisher €50,000
Mizen Tourism Funding (matching) €38,000

January 2006
First drawdown Fáilte Ireland/ERDF

January 2007
Second Drawdown Fáilte Ireland/ERDF

April 2007
Proposed completion of project and final drawdown
Total investment to date: . . . .€1,698,967 + €60,000 (Bridge)
This sum does not include monies invested by Mizen Tourism over the years from income.

Mizen Head Signal Station Visitor Centre has steady growth in numbers of visitors and income since its beginning 15 years ago. In 2007 there are 740 shareholders.

'Ready for the OFF'. Go-carting at Goleen Festival.

SHIPWRECKS AROUND OUR PARISH COASTLINE

Denis Downey

Whilst our parish coastline is renowned for its rugged scenery and sandy beaches, it also has a dark history as for the number of shipwrecks along the coast, especially from Crookhaven to the Three Castle Head. Having been the owner of land on both sides of Mizen Head, I grew up listening to stories of the wrecks of the *Queensmore*, the *Irada*, the *Oswestry* and many more from the older folk who witnessed many of these tragedies.

I have in my possession a cabin door from the *Memphis*, which was wrecked in Dunlough Bay on the 17th November 1896, which my late father remembered as a child. The biggest loss of life on our shores was from a ship called the *L'Impatiente* which was wrecked on 30th December 1796 on the south side of the Mizen Head near the present-day bridge leading to the lighthouse. Out of a total of 570 men, only seven survived. On the same ship, several hundred horses also perished.

In 1995 the *Irada* propeller was recovered from 40 metres of water off the Mizen Head. Reconnaissance and salvage preparation was carried out by divers. After some time, the 9-ton propellor was raised to the surface by the Irish light vessel *Granuaile* and is on display at Mizen Vision car park and is the centre of much attraction.

Most of the shipwrecks occurred from 1850 to 1910 highlighting the necessity for the erection of the lighthouse at Mizen Head. The following is some history of the various wrecks:

The Mizen Head. In less than 30 years there were seven shipwrecks and countless smaller craft whose loss was directly attributable to fog and the absence of a lighthouse on the Mizen Head, the nearest one being Fastnet.

The *Bohemian* was a three-year-old ship, her gross tonnage over 3,000 tons. She belonged to the Leyland Company of Liverpool and was engaged in the general carrying trade between America and

England. On Thursday 27th January 1881, she left Boston bound for Liverpool with about 2,500 tons of cargo on board, consisting of bales of cotton, barrels of flour, bacon apples, 70 head of cattle and a few pigs. Her crew consisted of 49 hands; and there were also on board four men working on the refrigerators, a cattle drover, two invalid sailors and a stowaway – in all, 57 souls.

The passage was a good one, the weather summer-like and nothing but a moderate easterly wind was experienced. All went well until she passed the Calf Light off the West Cork coast, and was on course for the Fastnet. Then fog began to settle down and the wind increased in strength from the southeast. The captain ordered the third officer (who was on the wheel at the time) to keep the vessel 'two points off' – meaning off the shore. The order was misunderstood and instead was kept two points off the wind. The engines were on half speed when the fog lifted slightly and the danger became immediately apparent to all on deck. The engines were put on full astern and were kept away for a full five minutes but to no avail – she struck a rock in Dunlough Bay, north of the Mizen Head.

The order was given to prepare the boats, of which there were three on board. The first boat was launched and five men got into it; but in less than a minute it was stove in owing to the rolling of the vessel on the rocks, and the men were drowned. Then the second boat was launched with five more men in it, but it, too, was stove in. This time the men were rescued by the four men in the third lifeboat, which had just been launched. Thirteen crew and a passenger clamoured aboard this lifeboat making the total on board 23 persons. Another small boat was launched to take off the captain and others but only three men had got into it when the ship lurched and the mainmast fell, striking the boat and sinking it. The men could not be found. The only boat left afloat then was the lifeboat with its 23 occupants. It pulled away from the *Bohemian* which moments later went down stern foremost in the angry waters, taking with it 35 men. In the lifeboat, the half-naked men (most of them had been in their bunks when the ship struck) tried to row in the dark but the cold was such that the oars soon slipped out of their numbed hands. For 12 hours they drifted. Two men died from exposure and were thrown overboard. The first sight of land came at daybreak and then all they saw were the cliffs of Dunmanus Bay (some 6 miles from the scene of the disaster). Fortunately, some people of the shore saw their plight and were able to get ropes to them and succeeded in pulling them ashore. They were brought to some houses where they were given food and clothing. While the men in the lifeboat were being pulled ashore, coastguards were looking out at the remains of the Bohemian. Three masts were still above water. Then a man was noticed on the rock at ten o'clock in the morning, but no attempt could be made to save him owing to the inaccessible nature of the place. The people on shore could see him bend his head as the waves washed over him and then when they receded he would wave his arms about avidly as a signal for assistance. The rocket apparatus was used to try to reach him. Two lines were fired over the rock but he was unable to reach either of them. Night fell and then at dawn the following morning he disappeared.

All that remained now was a bay full of wreckage and floating debris. Bales of cotton, bacon and barrels of flour were littered everywhere. As much as possible was salvaged but even here disaster sturck. A man trying to pick up a piece of bacon was drowned when a wave carried him off the rocks.

Three years later, on 10th November 1885, the *Iberian*, a 2,000-ton ship, sailed from Boston for Liverpool with cattle and a general cargo. She had a crew of 46 with three cattle men, three men in charge of refrigeration and two stowaways. Fifty-four persons all told. An ordinary winter passage was experienced and it was hoped that quick trip to Liverpool would be accomplished. On Friday the 20th, the sun was completely obscured by fog, so no sightings could be taken. The steamer, however, kept on her course. At midnight that night, the second mate went on his watch. It was foggy. At one time there was moonlight but the fog was so dense that, though a lookout was maintained, no danger was seen ahead. At ten minutes to 2 o'clock, the second mate summoned the captain on deck. The *Iberian* was then proceeding at 10 knots. The captain was not long on deck when the fog, lifting like a curtain, disclosed the land in front of them. The order to reverse engines was given and promptly responded to, but before the way of the steamer could be stopped, she glided on to the rocks at a point called Bird Island, near Three Castle Head. Efforts were made to back her off but without effect. Shortly after she struck, the forehold was reported full of water. The other parts of the steamer were free. She bumped heavily for a while owing to a ground swell, and finally settled with a starboard list. The boats were launched and the second mate was sent away in the first boat to land and telegraph for assistance. His boat left at 3 o'clock, but owing to the difficulties in landing and a fresh breeze blowing off the land, he did not succeed in getting ashore until 11 o'clock that Saturday morning.

Three other boats left the ship, the last man to leave being Captain Maxwell. One boat was swept out to sea but managed to make it into Crookhaven. No lives were lost.

On Sunday, the *Iberian* became a total wreck, having slipped off the rocks into deep water. Four years after the loss of the *Iberian* and eight since the *Bohemian*, the *Queensmore*, a brand new ship having just completed her maiden voyage across the Atlantic, sailed from Baltimore in the United States en route to Liverpool on 27th October 1889. She had 900 cattle on board, over 2,000 bales of cotton, 850 tons of copper matte, 60,000 bushels of wheat, lard, tobacco, flour and some organs. There were 77 persons on board, including two stowaways. All went well until Tuesday, 5th November, when a portion of the cargo in the hold of the vessel was discovered to be on fire. No evidence was ever discovered as to the cause of the fire, which apparently originated in bales of cotton, stowed near the air shaft. All hands set to work immediately and did their utmost to get it under control. Three days later it was still burning but now they were in sight of Cape Clear. Captain Frenery decided on running the vessel ashore and getting into the first harbour he met to save the lives of all on board. The fire became unbearably hot. The captain ordered that some of the cattle and a large number of bales of cotton should be jettisoned while making a last desperate effort to subdue the fire. But in the midst of a dense fog, he ran into Dunlough Bay and struck off the Bully Rock off the Three Castle Head. She drifted off this rock but was so badly holed that she sank soon afterwards in the middle of the bay in over 160 feet of water.

By then, fortunately, all had taken to the boats and so the disaster was free from loss of human life. Eleven bullocks were all that was saved of the livestock. Divers located the wreck some weeks later but expressed the opinion that there was no hope of salvaging her cargo.

And not before time, a strong general opinion was expressed that a fog station or lighthouse should be erected at either the Mizen or Three Castle Head.

Less than two months later another shipwreck, this time not a steamer but a large iron barque of over 1,000 tons register. The *Cherwell* sailed from Dundee in May 1888 to Newport in Wales, and thence to Mauritius with a cargo of coal.

From there she went to Brazil and then back again to Mauritius next to Ceylon, then to Calcutta and from there to the west coast of South America. Their next and last voyage was from Chile where they took on board a cargo of nitrate for Liverpool and were bound to Cobh for orders.

All went well until midnight of 31st December 1889, when the captain, not having seen the sun for five days, lost his bearings and ran into Dunlough Bar and struck the rocks beneath the Three Castle

Head. The ship rebounded off the rocks and a boat was quickly lowered and the crew, which consisted of 19 hands all told, stripped off their clothing and jumped into the water and from there they were able to scramble into the lifeboat. Two men did not jump, the first officer and an able seaman, and before they had another opportunity, the vessel sank head foremost, taking the two men with her.

The 17 men in the boat landed at Carbery Island in the dead of night but were unable to find a house. They had to wait until morning before they could make for the mainland of Dunmanus and find food and shelter.

On 18 November 1896, the *Memphis* struck rocks no more than 500 yards from the *Bohemian* and again in foggy conditions. She was a vessel of 3,000 tons gross and was sailing from Montreal to Bristol with a general cargo and 380 head of cattle. Four men were lost when a lifeboat capsized, five were drowned from rocks, which seven men reached the instant the steamer struck by getting over her bow, and two were lost in their endeavour to get ashore by ropes. Another lifeboat, with 21 men on board, landed in Dunmanus Bay while three who climbed the masthead were rescued after the experience of clinging nine hours to the masthead rigging. Thus out of a total of 47 persons on board the ship, 11 were lost. The ship was a total wreck.

During a dense fog on Sunday morning, 17th March 1899, the steamship *Oswestry* of 1,560 tons, was wrecked in Dunlough Bay. The sea was calm and they were going at average speed because of the fog when the crew realised their perilous position, but it was too late. The moment the vessel struck the rock, the engines were reversed but to no avail. There was not the slightest panic on board; 12 got away in a lifeboat while the others were rescued from the shore.

By the next day, Monday, the stern had sunk in 60 feet of water, the hatches were washed off and the cargo was floating out. On Tuesday nothing could be seen of the ship but the forecastle. Salvage work on the cargo of shipwrecks named so far had been too difficult to attempt because of their position and depth. The *Oswestry* was in much different prospect. Though her stern lay in almost 120 feet of water, her bows and midships were in only 60 feet. Salvage work by divers began immediately. By 18th March, less than a week since the ship was wrecked, 260 bales of cotton and 25 tons of copper had been recovered. Bad weather stopped operations periodically, but work continued for a month. By then, all floatable cargo had gone and efforts were made to salvage some of the 10,000 steel billets in the hold. Reports of operations ceased in June when explosives caused the ships to fall in on the cargo.

From 1896 onwards, frequent representations were made to the Irish Light Commissioners as to the necessity of establishing a fog signal on Mizen Head. This body absolutely refused to erect the station, and the Board of Trade, having no power to compel them to do so, or to erect such a station themselves, the matter was referred to Trinity House, and eventually in 1906, ten years after the first representations were made, the Irish Lights Commissioners were directed by Trinity House to proceed with the erection of the fog-signal station. By 1908, work was well under way on the very tip of the Mizen Head. But the Mizen was to have its grand finale. It began in 1906 with the loss of the *Ribble*, a trawler, and then in 1908 another trawler, the *Manoes*, was lost underneath the Head.

On 5th December 1908, the *Irada* sailed from Galveston, Texas, with a cargo of cotton valued at over £250,000. She was steaming to Liverpool. Fine weather favoured the passage up until the 15th, when bad weather set in. Heavy seas started to roll and fog banks were experienced on reaching the Irish coast; the weather then became quite thick and it was impossible for the navigator to get a bearing. The fog grew thicker and then half an hour after midnight, the fine liner struck on the rocks a few yards from the mainland.

Four minutes after striking, the engine room was flooded and, in a few more minutes, the vessel parted amidships. Captain Roberts with the first officer was on the bridge and immediately had the boats launched, and then discovered how close they were to the mainland, a sheer cliff almost 400 feet in height. The crew scrambled on to ledges of the rock as best they could. Shortly after the ship struck, some of the men lowered the stewardess, the only woman on board, with ropes from the ship's side, with the intention of putting her ashore. But a that moment the ship chose to roll on its side and in so doing crushed the girl. Four able seamen and the captain were lost in a similar manner.

Eight hours later, workmen on the fog-signal station saw the cargo floating about and then noticed the crew clinging to the side of the cliff. Ropes were lowered and 63 of the men were hauled up the cliff. Of the disaster, the Marine Insurance Market in London said that it was one of the heaviest blows that had ever fallen upon underwriters of marine insurance risks. The next era of shipwreck losses on our south Irish coast was due to an entirely different cause and that was World War I.

The Ballad of the Memphis

When the Memphis, she left Montreal, the weather it was fine
Said the captain to his officers we'll have a merry time
But coming towards the Irish coast there fell a heavy fog
And the captain lost his bearing through an error in the log

On the 14th of November at 10 o'clock that night
A lookout on the forecastle head he thought he saw a light
We took it to be the Fastnet Rock but sorry am I to say
It was through that fatal error we got wrecked in Dunlough Bay

When the Memphis struck the rock that night, our captain he did say
Brave boys, she'll go to pieces and we'll be cast away
So lower your life boats quickly and try your lives to save
And pray sweet God that none of us will meet a watery grave

So they lowered the starboard lifeboat and quickly she was manned
And before she reached the waterline the aftertackle jammed
The fore one then went by the run and the boat she swung around
The crew got in the water and four of them were drowned

Now the other boat was safely lowered, the painter was made fast
The crew were getting into her, the captain was the last
But another sea came rolling down and swept our boat away
That left our captain to his fate that night in Dunlough Bay

But the captain of the Memphis had courage stout and brave
He jumped on to the rigging, his precious life to save
But in the act of doing so another sea came on
And swept our captain overboard, he thought his end had come

Now the captain of the Memphis had a luck for him in store
He jumped on to a bullock's back and was safely brought ashore
Where he was kindly treated by the neighbours there next day
And that, my friends, concludes my song of the wreck in Dunlough Bay

Cork/West Mizen

La Solidada

The Spanish frigate sank at Crookhaven on 25th January 1780. The ship had been taken as a prize by a Liverpool privateer.

Sailor Prince

After the storm of February 1874, the barque, *Sailor Prince*, was offered for sale as a wreck on 3rd March 1874. The 445-ton vessel was built at St John New Brunswick in 1862. She was offered for sale as seen at anchor at the coastguard station at Crookhaven. In addition 2,000 Havana sugar boxes were for sale.

Huntingdon

The *Huntingdon* was wrecked on rocks at Spanish Island, Baltimore, on 6th November 1758. The ship had come from Zante with a cargo of currants, which were saved. The master was Thomas Erasmus.

Cork Mizen

Broad Oak

The 274-ton sailing ship Broad Oak was wrecked at Dunlough Bay on 29th December 1852. She carried cotton and sugar from Pernambucco to Liverpool. The captain and 15 of the crew were lost as they tried to scramble ashore on to the rocks, or were washed away. The mate and four sailors were saved by Mr Simmons, a local magistrate who rushed to the scene with the police.

Taurima

On 3rd August 1985, the pleasure trawler Taurima owned by the then-leader of the opposition, Mr Charles Haughey, was wrecked when it struck just below the lighthouse at Mizen Head. All aboard were saved with the help of the lightkeepers. Some wreckage lies at 15 metres in the deep inlet in the Head. As the vessel was wooden, little is left.

Prudence

On 13th February 1881, the 148-ton schooner *Prudence* was wrecked on the south-west coast. She was built of oak at Bedford and owned by Mssrs White Bros of Waterford. She was carrying oats from Limerick to London. Her master Mr Thomas and crew were lost.

Memphis

The 3,191-ton 345-foot *Memphis* of the African SS Co was wrecked at

Dunlough Bay near Mizen Head on 17th November 1896. The Dominon Line had chartered the ship from Elder Dempster Line. She was en route from Montreal to Avonmouth carrying timber, flour, bacon, butter, cattle and general cargo, which included lead ingots. She was built by Harland and Wolf in 1890. Nine of the crew were lost. Some escaped by the boats while the engineers climbed the rigging. One boat capsized. A local family, the Learys, took out a boat from Aughmina and saved some of the crew. Evan Jones of Carnavonshire, who lost his life in the shipwreck, is buried at the Church of Ireland cemetery at Crookhaven. The remains of the ship lie in 24 metres near a rock outcrop (Carraig na Coose) on the south side of the bay. They are well scattered with only the boiler and anchors readily identifiable.

Iberian

The *Iberian* was wrecked on 21st November 1885 in Duncannon Bay just on the coast half a mile south of Bird Island near Mizen Head. She was en route from Boston to Liverpool when she encountered thick weather and ran on the rocks. She had obtained no bearing the previous day. The vessel carried a cargo of cattle. The crew of 54 escaped in four boats, three of which landed on the rocks while the fourth was found after some time. The vessel broke up in the storm of 15th October 1896.

Oswestry

The 2,419-ton 300-foot *Oswestry* owned by Sivewright Bacon & Co was wrecked at Mizen Head on 12th March 1899. She was en route from Newport News and Norfolk Va. to Manchester with cotton, deal, copper ingots, iron plates, bars and Indian corn. The ship was built by E Withy & Co at Hartlepool in 1888. The wreck occurred in fog just south of a rock pinnacle in the small bay on the north side of Mizen Head. Captain Wilson and the crew of 24 landed safely with assistance from locals by scaling the rocky outcrops. The ship broke in two, releasing the cargo, and only the forepart was visible. Mr Swanton, the Lloyds agent, organised boats to salvage the cotton aboard. The *Oswestry* was built in 1888 by Furness at Hartlepool. A local farmer saved an engineer by carrying him on his back up the cliff. As a mark of gratitude, the farmer received gifts from him each time he reached port.

Bohemian

The 3,052-ton 400-foot steamer *Bohemian* left Boston for Liverpool on 27th January 1881 with a cargo of cotton and bacon. On Sunday

6th February she ran into thick weather though the sea was calm. At 8pm she passed the Calf Light with was visible, but at 1am on the 7th, the ship struck on a reef of rocks running out from Caher Island off Mizen Head. Though the helm was put hard a port and the engines reversed, the vessel sank in 35 metres so that only her masts showed. Captain Grundy and 35 of the crew of 57 were lost. The *Bohemian* was built at Harlands in 1870 and owned by F Leyland & Co.

Augusta

The *Augusta*, a 136-foot iron steamer of 54 tons was built at Swansea in 1849 and acquired by Messrs Hodder and Co of Cork in 1881. She was totally wrecked in Dunmanus Bay on 5th December 1886.

Mountaineer

On 14th December 1850 the *Mountaineer* was grounded at Dunmanus Bay. She left Quebec on 9th November with timber, commanded by Robert Harrisson. A severe gale drove her into the bay. She anchored to ride out the storm close to Carbery Island but was close to the rocks at Kitchen Cove. The next day the coastguards went out to the endangered vessel and she cut anchors and beached on the mud beneath the coastguard station thus saving the crew.

Ranger

The brig *Ranger* of North Shields was wrecked on the rocks at Dunmanus Bay on 30th March 1850. Commanded by John Robertson she carried Egyptian wheat to Cork or Falmouth for orders.

Caroline

The 40-ton cutter *Caroline* was wrecked in Dunmanus Bay on 15th October 1886. The six aboard escaped. She was en route from Crookhaven to Dunmanus Bay on salvage work.

Irada

On 22nd December 1908 the *Irada*, en route from Galveston to Liverpool with a cargo of cotton, was wrecked on Mizen Head. The ship was built by JH Wellsford & Co in 1900 and measured 8,124 tons and 501 feet in length. She was one of the largest vessels of her time. The accident occurred during a SW gale and fog. The Bull Light was seen but its distance miscalculated. The Fastnet Light was not visible. The strong ebb tide caused the vessel to strike shore and become wedged between a rock pinnacle and the mainland at the small bay near Mizen Head. As some of the crew scrambled ashore on a rope, a sea caught the vessel and heeled over, crushing a stewardess and the mate. The captain, who had remained last, was not seen after this mishap. Most of the crew escaped in the ship's boats and landed at Crookhaven. Captain Arthur Wellesley Roberts of Brikdale, Lancashire, is buried at the Church of Ireland cemetery at Crookhaven. Four crewmen and a stewardess were also lost out of a total of 69. Two are buried at Old Kilmore graveyard. The survivors were assisted up the cliffs by the Irish Lights workers constructing the fog station at Clohane Island. The cargo valued at £250,000 included 21,000 bales of cotton. The hull was insured for £896,000. It was washed ashore at Paleen Harbour, two miles west of Castletownbere. The Lloyds agent at Bere, Mr McCarthy, contacted Captain Hugh Williams, the owner's representative. The *Perserverance* was chartered from Scotts of Queenstown and much cargo recovered and transferred to a larger steamer for transport to Liverpool.

Confiance

On 21st August 1822, the 393-ton brig sloop *Confiance* was wrecked between Mizen and Three Castle Head. Commander Morgan and all 100 aboard were lost. The fifth rate carried 36 guns. Cannon were located near the small landing at Coosacuslaun during a search for an Austrian drowning victim about 1980. It is believed that these come from the *Confiance*.

L'Impatiente

One of the 43 ships of the French fleet which accompanied Wolf tone from Brest to Bantry was wrecked near Mizen Head. The expeditionary force commanded by vice admiral Morard de Galle was storm-bound in Bantry Bay and set out on its return journey to France. On 30th December 1796 the fregate-bombardiere *L'Impatiente* was wrecked on the south side of Mizen Head near the spectacular bridge to the lighthouse. There were only seven survivors from the crew of 560 commanded by Captain de Vaisseau Deniau. *L'Impatiente* was armed with 20 or 21 cannon (24 livre) and a mortar. Three anchors, 10 large and one small cannon, lie at 15–20 metres just out from the rocks near the steps at Coosanisky. Mortar shot, ballast and other wreckage lies about the area. The victims were buried in the sands at Barleycove. *L'Impatiente* was built at Lorient in 1794–5. Two further vessels of the fleet were lost, the frigate la Surveillante at Bantry Bay and the ship of the line Scevola foundered out to sea from Mizen Head.

Ribble

On 26th May 1906, the 71-ton steam trawler *Ribble* struck near Mizen Head in fog and sunk. The wreck occurred on Clohane Island under the fog station construction site. The 183-ton trawler was built in 1900 and operated from Fleetwood by Wyre Steam Trawling Co. The captain, crew of eight and two passengers were saved.

Manaos

The 82-ton steam trawler *Manaos* of Milford struck Clohane Island off Mizen Head on 1st October 1908 having been built at Shields for Hancock and Harris of Milford. The trawler was returning in fog from fishing off the Blaskets when she struck in a cleft on the Island. She became wedged at the foot of a cliff on one side and a shelf on the other. Skipper Salter and eight of the crew reached the rock shelf with the aid of a plank and a rope. The mate Charles McKenna was drowned. After ten hours, Thomas Lord the foreman of the workers on the construction of the fog station led a team of rescuers who saved the survivors.

Cherwell

The 1,129-ton 204-foot iron barque *Cherwell* struck the rock at Three Castle Head in Dunlough Bay on 31st December 1889. She had carried coal from Newport to Mauritius and loaded nitrate at Pisagua in Chile bound to Cork for orders. The wreck occurred at the rocks under Three Castle Head. After 115 days at sea, Captain F Toole had no sun sight for five days due to fog. A boat was lowered and 17 of the 19 crew escaped. The first officer and a seaman were lost when the ship went down head foremost. The survivors landed at Carbery Island and waited the night before they could reach the mainland. She was built by Middlesboro in 1863 and owned by Edward Bates of Liverpool.

Queensmore

On 8th November 1889 the *Queensmore* ran on to Bully Rock in Dunlough Bay. She had sailed to the US on her maiden voyage and was returning from Baltimore to Liverpool. The ship carried 900 cattle, 2,000 bales of cotton, 850 tons of copper ore and 1,000 tons of wheat, as well as 77 passengers, crew and stowaways. Her cargo of cotton spontaneously ignited which was a common occurrence due to heating. Despite three days of fire fighting, the fire still raged. Captain Frenery decided on the normal course of action in these dire circumstances, to run the ship on a sandy shore and flood the holds. Though Cape Clear was sighted, a fog descended and he ran into Dunlough.

Thalia

The *Thalia* went ashore and was bulged at Crookhaven on 5th February 1822. She was from Savannah for Liverpool, captained by Butler. The cargo was saved.

Unknown

An unnamed vessel from the Brazils was wrecked at Crookhaven in early February 1813. She carried bales of cotton.

Leander

The *Leander* was wrecked on rocks near Mizen on 18th December 1824. She was from New Orleans for Liverpool, captained by Fisher. The crew were all saved.

Arum

The transport *Arum* went ashore and was damaged on 14th January 1814 at Crookhaven.

Marchioness Abercorn

On 19th November 1849, the 875-ton *Marchioness Abercorn* was wrecked at Mizen. The ship was bound for Cardiff from Quebec.

Ranger

On 4th April 1850, the *Ranger* was wrecked in Dunmanus Bay. She was bound for Queenstown from Malta.

Whim

On 30th October 1852 the *Whim* was lost off Mizen. She was bound from Ayr to Cardiff.

Calypso

On 26th February 1848, the 370-ton *Calypso* was lost off Mizen.

Mary

The 191-ton *Mary* of Dublin was lost a Crookhaven in 1833.

Tarlton

The *Tarlton* went ashore and was lost at Crookhaven on 9th November 1762. She was captained by Picker. The voyage was Jamaica to Liverpool.

Unknown

A large ship from the West Indies was wrecked at Crookhaven on 24th December 1794. All aboard were lost.

Dara

A wreck just west of the lighthouse at Crookhaven is described locally as the *Dara*. There are no further details about the type or date of the loss.

Wolverine

On 17th March 1867 the *Wolverine* was wrecked near the lighthouse at Crookhaven. The 485-ton wooden barque had put into Crookhaven for provisions but was dragged from her anchors and smashed on the rocks. The crew of 15 and Master Alexander Ryle were saved by the coastguards.

Providence

The *Providence* ran on rocks at Crookhaven and sank on 11th December 1817. She was bound for St Michael's from Plymouth, captained by Power.

Weazel

The *Weazel* was lost at Crookhaven on 16th March 1784. She ws from Tortola for Liverpool, commanded by Melling.

Brass cannon

A 'brass' cannon was found on a diving trip near Mizen Head. It is not clear what ship it may have come from. It is unlikely that *L'Impatiente* carried bronze guns, as her cannon were iron. The location of the gun or any accurate description is unavailable.

La Soldida

It is attractive to associate Spanish Point near Crookhaven with the frigate *La Soldida*, recorded as lost at Crookhaven, but nothing has been found underwater at the site. The Spanish frigate sank 25th January 1780. One local story said that a ship had beached near Spanish Point for repairs.

Trio

25th February 1827, Bexfield, Dunlough Bay, Derry

Try Again

11th September 1828, Crookhaven, Quebec, auctioned.

Barbara

25th November 1829, Denis Casey, south side of Crookhaven, Berehaven.

Elizabeth

The *Elizabeth* was wrecked at Crookhaven on 25th August 1767. Mr French, a customs boatman, claimed for his salvage services.

Liberty

On 8th November 1877, the 10-ton smack *Liberty* was lost three quarters of a mile, north-west of Mizen Head. The Liberty was 19 years old and owned by W Roan of Arklow.

Hope

13th February 1823, Middleton, Ballyrisode, Crookhaven, Newry.

John Campbell

1st December 1831, Patterson, Crookhaven, Cork, auctioned. The *John Campbell* was wrecked at the entrance to Crookhaven on 15th December 1831. She was bound for Cork from Quebec. The crew were saved. Her captain was Campbell.

Goleen iin the 1930s.

GOLEEN VILLAGE

by Geraldine Camier

The village of Goleen grew up mainly in the second half of the nine-teenth century to serve the needs of the hinterland. Prior to this, Ballydevlin was the main settlement. It must have been a hamlet of some antiquity, as the little bridge spanning the stream near what is now The Heron's Cove is a clapper bridge built without arches, but with stone flags. Apparently there is, or was, an inscription on it as fol-lows: 'Cain O'Mahony, lacking bricks, built me in 1646'. Why Ballydevlin died as a village and Goleen rose and thrived is possibly due to the more level terrain on the Goleen side.

Until the middle of the nineteenth century Goleen contained a con-stabulary barracks (which was destroyed during the Civil War), a church built in 1806, Goleen House, the seat of J McCarthy Esq, and few other buildings. It is not known what the population of Goleen vil-lage was at this time, although the population of the area known as Kilmoe was 6,889 in 1837 – this included approximately 600 children divided between public and private schools, and presumably more who were not of school-going age. As the number of children as a pro-portion to the population as a whole seems small, there must have been many who did not attend school at all. Presumably, the cata-clysmic event that was the Famine made a big dent in this population, both from death and from emigration.

By 1914 Goleen was a thriving village, practically self-sufficient. Coastal steamers landed goods to supply the many businesses in the village, which included a bakery, several vintners, a fish monger, a shoemaker, several grocers and drapers, a blacksmith, a boatbuilder, carpenters and general contractors and presumably a butcher. There were two hotels: McCormacks where the Lobster Pot now stands and McCarthys where Denny O'Meara's Bar is now situated. The names over these businesses included Harrington, Love, McCarthy, Mahony, Scully, Sullivan, Ward, Wilkinson and Barnett. There was a Dispensary under the auspices of Dr Thomas Neville, assisted by

District Nurse Ellen O'Brien; a Registry run by G McCormack; a Petty Sessions Court every fourth Friday where the clerk was Samuel Whitley; the Constabulary Barracks where Sgt Michael Madden was in charge. There were two schools – Joseph O'Driscoll was head of the Roman Catholic School, which is still going, and George Ross was head of the Church of Ireland school, which has been closed probably since the late fifties or early sixties. Spiritual matters were taken care of by the Rev J McCarthy, CC, and by Rev WH Brew.

Over the following decades there was a gradual decline in the fortunes of Goleen, as there was in the country as a whole. The area endured poverty throughout the thirties, forties and fifties in the day before social welfare and the EU. Emigration stripped Goleen and its hinterland of its youth, who went to Britain to help rebuild after World War II, and also to America and Australia. Now it's choice as much as necessity, the desire for experience of foreign climes, that motivates the young to go to America, Australia and elsewhere. There has also been the phenomen of immigration to the area; young couples who – disillusioned with big city life – want to bring up families here where it is safe. We have to welcome any development that helps to increase our still declining population.

Since the seventies, maybe even a little before then, Goleen has become a tourist destination, although the nature of this tourism too has changed. We are now a destination for the well-heeled, who do not rent accommodation but prefer to buy it. In an area where farming and fishing were traditionally the mainstay of the population and emigration took care of surplus people, we are now, for a few short months of every year, a tourists' play-ground. This means welcome employment for the families of those who still farm and, increasingly less, fish in Goleen. Many farmers now earn extra money in the building trade, as small farms are no longer viable. While we still have pubs and other businesses in the village, I think it would be fair to say that they struggle to compete with the supermarkets and off-licences of the larger towns. The fair day has given way to the mart, and prosperity has given people more mobility. It seems that the facts of life conspire against small villages everywhere, including Goleen. Like many coastal villages, Goleen has more houses than ever and fewer permanent residents every year.

GOLEEN PARISH HALL

Ellen Scully

Fr Daniel J McCarthy was curate in Goleen from 1923 to 1928 and during those years he was responsible for the building of the parish hall. Voluntary work was responsible for most of the labour; only two workmen received wages. They were Jerry and Paddy Coughlan, Balteen. On completion the cost of maintaining the hall was met by the profits of dances, annual concerts, whist drives, etc. In later years the profits were donated to defray church repairs.

In the early 1950s the hall had a licence to hold 18 dances yearly from 9 p.m. to 2 a.m., and patrons should be over 18 years. The first chairman was Fr Timothy O'Sullivan, PP, Fr J McCarthy was secretary and treasurer, Ricky Collins was licencee and held the position until 1968. The committee included Dr Thomas Neville, Denis Cullinane, Denis Donovan.

In 1968 Michael McCarthy took over as licencee and remained so until replaced by Pat McCarthy, Gurthdove, in 1990. The refurbishment of the parish hall was completed in 1999. Finance for these improvements was donated from parish funds. The parish priest at that time was Fr Denis Cashman.

The committee put a lot of time and effort into this project. Committee was as follows: Jimmy Downey, chairperson; Breda Buckley, secretary; Elizabeth Barry, treasurer; Noreen Hurley, Kathleen Downey, Miriam Goggin, Sheila Lucey, Michael Barry, Paul Sheehan and Pat McCarthy.

The hall is continually used since by the following: céilí classes, Retired Persons' Club, St Joseph's Young Priests Society, Scór na bPáistí, Scór na nÓg, the Pioneer Association, the GAA, School Sports Committee, Community Council, IFA, Community Alert, Mizen Rovers, kiddies' disco, bingo, etc. The present hall committee is as follows: Fr John O'Donovan, chairperson; Breda Buckley, Secretary; Elizabeth Barry, treasurer; Ellen Scully; ass. treasurer; Pat McCarthy, licencee; Jimmy Downey, caretaker; Donal Donovan, Michael Barry, Sheila Lucey, Mary Sheehan and Sheila Barnett.

Ode to Paddy Downey

There are those who make their names through sport
and others at the bar
And those of screen and radio, we sometimes call them stars
And we once had a General whose fame was based on crimes
But none can hold a candle to bould Downey of The Times.

We have all heard of Mick Mackey and of Kerry's Mick O'Dwyer
And Cavan's John Joe Reilly, who played the game with fire
And Ring, O'Connell, Meagher and Meath's mighty man Mick Lyons
But none can hold a candle to bould Downey of The Times.

'Tis a pleasure for to see him with his goalposts by his side
His lion's mane of silver hair and his big Cork arms thrown wide
A glass of créatur in his hand, from his pipe the sweet smoke climbs
You won't meet company finer than bould Downey of The Times.

If you want to talk of poetry, then Downey is your man
Or sport or life or music or life's eternal plan
Or why the Dubs miss penalties or a view on Spanish wines
He's a walking bloody library is our Downey of The Times.

Had he been born a racehorse then he would be Red Rum
Or had he been a football team, then Kerry eighty-one
He's the Rolls Royce of his class that man, the champagne of drink
lines
A shockin' dacent fellow is bould Downey of The Times.

He did not forget the working class when times were lean and mean
He made the bosses shudder cos his mind was sharp and keen.
No middle class persuasion here, he drew the battle lines
An officer and gentleman is Downey of The Times.

And when the great ref in the sky, He blows his whistle long
We know that our friend Paddy will join that happy throng
And get a real All-Star award from that last save on the line
But until then enjoy yourself, bould Downey of The Times.

– by Sean McConnell and Eugene McEldowney

GOLEEN COMMUNITY PLAYGROUP LTD

by *Mary Sheehan*

From where it all began to today

Back in 1992 a group of mothers met up and decided that a parent and toddler group was needed in the area. They hired the parish hall and advertised and every Tuesday morning from 10 a.m. to 1 p.m. seven or eight mums with their toddlers came along. Over the next couple of years it expanded and as these children got older the parents felt that playschool was needed to span the gap between parent and toddler group and primary school. Playschool was then started on Wednesday and Friday mornings. Initially playschool was started with a mothers' rota, two on each morning. Then after a while, to give more consistency, one of the mothers agreed to become a permanent play leader with the other mums continuing with the rota.

As the group expanded in numbers, so did our equipment, and as the parish hall was used by other clubs and organisations, after each session everything had to be packed away. A premises was needed where everything could be left in place for the next session. Over the next few years several different locations were used that were very kindly put at the disposal of the group. A porta-cabin in Barleycove Caravan Park was used for a few years. Nottages Bar in Crookhaven, which closed for the winter, was used for one term. The games room at Barleycove hotel was used for another term and then it was the sailing club in Crookhaven.

The group was very grateful for all these places, but all of them had to be vacated for the summer. Storage then had to be found for all the equipment, which resulted in the equipment being distributed between all of the parents' houses. Another major problem was that none of these premises passed the regulations set out for the running of a playgroup; they were not built for this purpose.

Following an inspection by the Southern Health Board in the spring of 1998 the group was being told to find alternative premises and also the advice being given to the group was to find a suitable building in the area or to build a new purpose built building. The AGM was held in June 1998 and the following committee was elected: chairperson, Vicki Evans; secretary, Bernie Griffin Sheehan; treasurer, Mary Sheehan; PRO, Dawn Little; Norma O'Driscoll, Mary Donovan, Jan Harrington and Judi Ann Riley. At the committee's first meeting it was decided to look into the options of a suitable building in the area, or a suitable site – would it have to be bought, could it be leased or would someone be so kind as to donate a site? With £432 in the bank it was hard to imagine what is today. Having researched the two options, there was no suitable building available. Some ground that was for sale in the area also proved non-productive.

Letters were written to the local councillors in connection with a plot of ground in the possession of Cork County Council that was not being used. After a succession of meetings, on 21st September 1998 Cork County Council sanctioned a site for a playschool building in Goleen. On the legal side it took from then until June 2000 before work could commence on the site. However, the committee set to work on other matters, they met with architect Jim Leahy in relation to getting plans drawn up and having them submitted to County Hall for planning permission.

Sharon Walsh, a fire consultant/engineer, was met with in relation to preparing a fire certificate application. Plans were sent in to County Hall in February 1999. Correspondence from County Hall stated that a limited company would need to be formed to satisfy the legal requirements. Local solicitor Paul O'Sullivan set to work to get the company formed and this was complete in July 1999. A long-term lease for 66 years on the site also had to be drawn up and Paul also set this up. Copies of the plans were sent to all the local builders for quotations, to building contractors and to individuals who operate the direct labour system.

In November of 1999 the committee decided on the builders and opted to go with the direct labour system involving three individuals: Eamonn Sheehan was in charge of the site work, foundations and floor, footpaths, sewer connection preparation and fencing around the building on completion, John O'Driscoll would do the block work and plastering, and Tim Supple would do the roof and carpentry. Going with this system meant more work for the committee, as regards all the other workers, like the electrician and the plumber, quotations for windows, kitchen and presses, a tiler and tile prices, floor covering, paint and electrical appliances, tarmac and fencing. On the other hand, dealing directly with the different companies gave the committee more scope to get sponsorship and discount.

As well as sorting all this out the committee had been researching grants and funding available. There was also ongoing local fundraising to which a very generous local community was never found wanting. Approximately one third of the total cost was raised locally and the remaining funds in grant aid from the Southern Health Board, The People in Need Trust, Cork County Council and Leader.

In July of 2000 work started on the site and after eight months of very hard work and the setback of the roof being blown off in a storm in November of 2000, the dream became a reality and opened in April of 2001, the building opened for playschool three mornings and for parent and toddler one morning weekly.

The playschool was officially opened by Paddy Sheehan, TD, on 10th August 2001 Along with Eamonn Sheehan, John O'Driscoll and Tim Supple the following is a list of people and companies involved in the building: Denny O'Donoghue, (plant hire) completed the site work; Drimoleague Concrete, concrete and blocks; Munster Joinery, fitted the windows and doors; Ger Minihane, completed the electrical work; Michael Walsh, (plumbing suppliers); Tim Sheehan, completed plumbing; Carbery Timber, supplied roofing materials; Drinagh Co-Op, various building materials; Clonakilty Tiles, tiles; Rachel Manahan, tiling; Kellys of Bantry, flooring; Clohane Wood Products, kitchen and presses; Global Trading (Cork), paint; O'Driscolls Electricial, electricial equipment; HMS (Donal Hourihane), fire extinguishers; Tuf-Mac Tarmacadam, tarmac; Celtic Mats (Longford), safety mats; Ardtec, Drimoleague, fencing; Justin Doody, painter; Mizen Landscaping, landscaping.

In 2000 the Department of Justice Equality and Law Reform introduced capital grants for playschool facilities and also staffing grants. The building was in place and running and there was not a loan in place to be paid back; in fact at any stage of the project a loan was not needed. The committee applied for the staffing grant and in August of 2002 was granted a staffing grant for one year. This meant playschool was now open four mornings and parent and toddler group continued on Tuesday mornings.

Two playleaders were employed to work each morning Jan Harrington and Judi Ann Riley. They both had completed the NCVA level 2 (now FETAC) certificate in childcare as required. The grant was reapplied for and in December 2003, after much perseverance, a grant of €64,000 was granted for two years on condition that an after-school club be set up. Since January 2004 Vicki Evans, and joined in April by Catherine O'Driscoll, have very successfully run the after-school club. Vicki and Catherine both have their FETAC certificate in childcare. The activities hosted by the after-school club have been many – baking, knitting and sewing, table tennis, jewellery making, clay and pottery making, drama, singing, set dancing, art and crafts, model making, salsa dancing, woodwork, fit kids.

Another condition of the staffing grant was that the premises remain for 45 weeks of the year. A summer club has been run for the month of July, which has been very successful with the visitors to the area. The staffing grant was again renewed in December of 2005 for a further two years to the end of 2007 and hopefully it will again be renewed. Five people are currently employed: Judi Ann Riley, Jan Harrington, Sarah Hopkinson, Vicki Evans and Catherine O'Driscoll and the building is being used five days weekly from 9.30 p.m. to 5 p.m.

Even though the staffing grant is in place, a certain amount of fundraising is still needed to cover annual running costs like ESB, phone, heating, rates, water, refuse, insurance and replacing of equipment. Goleen Community Playgroup Ltd holds its AGM in November each year. There must be seven members on the board of directors.

Committee 1998–1999: chairperson, Vicki Evans; secretary, Bernie Griffin Sheehan; treasurer, Mary Sheehan; PRO, Dawn Little; Norma O'Driscoll, Mary Donovan, Jan Harrington, Judi Ann Riley.

Committee 1999–2000: chairperson, Vicki Evans; vice-chairperson, Dawn Little; secretary, Bernie Griffin Sheehan; treasurer, Mary Sheehan; PRO, Norma O'Driscoll; director, Jan Harrington; director, Judi Ann Riley.

Committee 2000–2001: chairperson, Vicki Evans; vice-chairperson, Dawn Little; secretary, Bernie Griffin Sheehan; treasurer, Mary Sheehan; PRO, Norma O'Driscoll; director, Jan Harrington; director, Alison O'Sullivan.

Committee 2001–2002: chairperson, Vicki Evans; vice-chairperson, Alison O'Sullivan; secretary, Rachel Manahan; treasurer, Amanda Thomas; PRO, Diana Hawkes; director, Bernie Griffin Sheehan; director, Dawn Little.

Committee 2002–2003: chairperson, Alison O'Sullivan; vice-chairperson, Anne Murnane; secretary, Rachel Manahan; treasurer, Amanda Thomas; PRO, Liz Flatman; director, Maura O'Reilly; director, Bernie Griffin Sheehan.

Committee 2003–2004: chairperson, Alison O'Sullivan; vice-chairperson, Anne Murnane; secretary, Maura O'Reilly; treasurer,

Rachel Manahan; PRO, Liz Flatman; director, Bernie Griffin Sheehan; director, Amanda Thomas.

Committee 2004–2005: chairperson, Alison O'Sullivan; vice-chairperson, Dawn Little; secretary, Bridget Whooley; treasurer, Rachel Manahan; PRO, Maura O'Reilly; director, Bernie Griffin Sheehan; director, Anne Murnane.

Committee 2005–2006: chairperson, Alison O'Sullivan; vice-chairperson, Jan Harrington; secretary, Bridget Whooley; treasurer, Rachel Manahan; PRO, Maura O'Reilly; director, Bernie Griffin Sheehan; director, Anne Murnane.

Committee 2006–2007: chairperson, Bernie Griffin Sheehan; vice-chairperson, Sherri Cullinane; secretary, Mary Sheehan; treasurer, Rachel Manahan; PRO, Liz Flatman; director, Joanne O'Driscoll; director, Miranda Van der Vlugt.

War Signal Station, Brow Head

TOM BARRY

by Denis Downey

When any of the older generation see the name Tom Barry on the page of any book, they will expect to read some story of the ambushes at Kilmichael, Upton or Crossbarry during the War of Independence masterminded by the legendary Tom Barry. Here in the parish of Goleen we had our own legend also by the name of Tom Barry, Cahir. Tom was born on 1st June 1896 and died on 3rd July 2003.

Tom broke many records and had many celebrations during the last ten years of his life, one having been the oldest male citizen in Ireland for the latter two and a half years of his life. I visited him on New Year's morning 2000. I wished him a happy new year and asked him how it felt to have started his third century, he paused for a few moments and then, with that roguish smile, said, 'Do you know I never felt the last one passing.'

Tom remembered standing outside his home on the evening of the 27th June 1904 waiting for darkness to fall so he could see the ray of light from the Fastnet Lighthouse, which was exhibited that night for the first time over the coastline and mountains of the parish. He saw the same light flashing for a further 99 years through good times and bad. He told me he saw the sailors from the Irada climbing the cliffs at Mizen Head as they floundered, when he was eleven years old. He walked to 7.30 mass on Christmas mornings, a round trip of 12 miles! He drank Guinness for two pence a pint when there were 240 pence in the pound. He outlived his mother by 95 years.

He had his first drive in a motor car with George Wilkinson when he was 45 years of age. He described the car as an old left-hand drive and a bit of a crock. He was ten years old when they decided to put a lighthouse on Mizen Head and he was shopping in Goleen when he heard of the death of Michael Collins. He was nineteen years of age and remembered the Saturday evening when the *Lusitania* was sunk off the Old Head of Kinsale in which his friend and neighbour John Coughlan and his daughter were lost. He was 20 years at the time of

60 Wedding Anniversary. The oldest male citizen in Ireland, Tom Barry with his wife Mai celebrating their Diamond Jubilee at 'Herons Cove' Restaurant on June 25th 2002. Mai is holding their Great Grand-son Adam, who is 105 years younger than Tom.

the Easter Rising and saw the Black and Tans in his native Cahir on a Sunday morning when they were searching for a few local volunteers, and again saw them questioning and searching people in Goleen village after mass that day. He was 25 years when he went to vote to elect our first native government. Tom was in his mid-seventies when he went to New-Bedford to see his sister. He said he enjoyed the trip and was not remotely fazed by the flight and the aeroplane.

When he started school, there were old people in every house who would have remembered the Famine. He said they were told very little about it, as those people wanted to put that dark period of history behind them, a stark contrast to the 150th anniversary when they were encouraged to learn the history of same. The 1st June 1996 was a special day in Tom's life, as he celebrated his 100th birthday. Mass was celebrated by Fr Cashman, PP, at eleven o'clock that Saturday morning and all his friends, neighbours and relatives were invited to attend. The celebrations went on until two or three o'clock the following morning and he was the last to retire. He got his cheque from the President that morning and gave the day answering the phone to well-wishers, his most important being two or three calls from his grand-daughter Linda in Australia.

Tom was 46 when he got married. His wife Mai was a neighbour's daughter and it's said he rocked her in the cradle. The 25th June 2002 was another special day for Tom and Mai; on that particular evening I met them both being driven by their daughter-in-law, Mary. After the usual handshake and asking how he was, he told me he was returning from Heron's Cove Restaurant where there was music and song and the best to eat and drink, so what could be wrong with him. I then asked him was there some special celebration? He paused for a few moments, 'I don't know,' he said, 'but they tell myself and that good lady in the back seat that we are married sixty years today.' I believe it's only one in every 6,000 to 7,000 couples are blessed to celebrate their diamond jubilee, and surely for a man that got married at 46 to celebrate his diamond jubilee 60 years later, should be one for the *Guinness Book of Records;* and this is why I said at the outset that we had our own legend here in Goleen parish in the person of Tom Barry.

Another eventful day in Tom's life was a celebration of the second phase development of the Mizen Vision project. He described the occasion as one of the happiest days of his life after the then Agriculture Minister, Joe Walsh, TD, had unveiled a board recording his longevity and made a special presentation to him. Paddy Sheehan, TD, was also present and said that Tom had worked hard and reared a family on a small holding north of the Mizen. 'We can't live on fresh air and cold water,' he said, but they are a significant factor, so now I think there might be a future for all of us, as they are the two things we have in abundance.

During the summer of 2000 a six-hour DVD was filmed on the life and times of Goleen parish and Tom gave a fifteen-minute interview in it of events in the early part of the last century. There is an old saying: 'All good things come to an end', and sadly for Tom it came in the form of a stroke which he suffered on 20th June 2003. He was moved to Bantry hospital and left his beloved Cahir for the last time. I went to see him in hospital but he was unconscious. It was sad to think that the voice that had told the stories of part of three centuries had gone silent at last.

He passed to his eternal reward on the 3rd July 2003 and was buried in Goleen two days later. May the sod of Goleen Church graveyard rest lightly on his gentle soul, we shall not see his likes again. *Go raibh deis De ar a annam.*

GOLEEN IFA

by Kieran O'Sullivan

The Irish Farmers Association, better known as the IFA, is the biggest farm organisation in the country. Its primary role is to defend farmers' rights and to fight and lobby for better prices and conditions for all types of farming, firstly at a national level, but now more than ever at the European and world stage. The IFA is a highly professional organisation whose record of delivery is the envy of many other representative bodies at home and in Europe. The organisation was set up in 1955 and was originally known as the NFA (National Farmers Association), but later changed its title to the IFA. The IFA is made up of 945 branches, which are at the lowest level of the organisation and they represent over 85,000 members.

Goleen, like many other parts of the country, set up a branch in the early years of the organisation, and, in fact, there were two branches in Goleen parish, as there was another branch over in Lowertown.

The Goleen branch was represented by people like Eugene Downing of Greenane and Donal O'Sullivan, Dunmanus. They voiced the concerns and problems of the members of the Goleen branch at the County Executive monthly meetings in Dunmanway. In the late 1950s–early '60s, times were tough for most farmers, with economic stagnation and low prices, and with the government of the day failing to listen to the NFA, it was decided that something major had to be done. In 1966 the organisation decided that they would march to Dublin to Dáil Éireann and demand better conditions for its members.

A big number of farmers from West Cork gathered in Bantry and set off for Dublin; while all the gathering marched out the road for a number of miles, a smaller representative group continued all the way to Dublin. There was one man from Goleen who walked all the way to Dublin, namely Eugene Downing. This was a marvellous achievement from a man from the most southwesterly point of Ireland, one that the Goleen branch and his family can always be proud of.

The Lowertown branch was represented by people like Willie King and their first chairman, Chris O'Sullivan, Bert Hunt, Tadhg O'Mahony, Declan O'Mahony and Connie Lucey. They, too, were very active in representing their fellow branch members and they also took part in the 1966 march. They were involved in the setting up of the West Cork Resources Survey, which was set up to get better conditions and improvements for West Cork farmers. Both branches represented the farmers of the parish for many years, but then they both went into a dormant state for over ten years, right through the 1980s and into the early 1990s, there was no branch here.

Then in the years 1994–1995, the West Cork Executive wanted to start up the Goleen branch again, so they sent Bernard O'Donovan, chairman of the West Cork Executive, along with Patrick Downey of Carrigmanus, to canvas new members for the local branch. A lot of new members joined the branch that year. There was a prize for the branch with the most new members and Patrick Downey won the prize, which was a trip to visit several different EU countries and to see the different types of farming carried on there.

Teddy Twomey and Patrick Downey were the two officers of the newly formed branch. They were succeeded in 1996 by Dick Burchill as chairman and Martin Sheehan as secretary. Joe Hurley was registrar and Pat Scully was treasurer. In 1998 Jerry Sheehan succeeded Pat Scully as treasurer. Richard Connell became the new chairman in 2001 and Gerard Donovan became registrar, after eight years as secretary, Martin Sheehan handed over the job to Derry Kennedy in 2004.

The present-day officers are: Kieran O'Sullivan, chairman; Derry Kennedy, secretary; Richard Connell, registrar, and Bernie Sheehan as the lady representative, which she has done for a number of years.

The present-day Goleen branch continues to represent the local farmers like the original branch did in the 1960s and 1970s, but it was in January and February of 2006 that the Goleen branch once more made itself known to the highest level of the organisation, like Eugene Downing did in 1966, when Richard Connell highlighted to the top people in the organisation and to the newly elected president Padraig Walshe, that there had been a major error made in agreeing with the Nitrates Directive as proposed by the Minister for the Environment. The directive was actually signed into law on 1st February 2006, but, after weeks of negotiating between the Minister of Agriculture and the IFA, the directive was changed and much fairer and more balanced law was put in place for the application of the chemical fertiliser. The change was almost soley brought about by the inital work done by

Richard Connell in the way he highlighted this very important and complex issue.

At the West Cork County Executive AGM in December 2006, Richard Connell was elected a County Executive officer to represent the Rural Development Section. He is the first Goleen branch member to be elected on the County Executive, which means the Goleen branch will be well known at national level.

The present-day branch has over 50 members, and is in a good, strong, healthy state – and long may it continue.

View of Crookhaven Village, 1930s.

FISHING BOATS OF CROOKHAVEN

by Billy O'Sullivan and Jerry O'Mahony

1929 Captain Trehue, then owner of the lobster ponds, brought three lobster fishing boats from France: *Trimordeur, Evgenie and Edmonde.*

1931 Another boat that fished for lobster off the west coast was the *Thrift*. She was lost in Crookhaven Harbour in 1939; sunk in a storm. Around the same time, Din, Jim and Tom O'Driscoll had boats fishing for lobster in summer and herring in winter, as did Dan O'Leary and Sean Flynn.

1932 The *Con Florrie* was built by Tom Gainey for John Florrie O'Driscoll. The O'Driscolls of Rock Street had a boat and engine around the same time.

1939–45 The O'Sullivans had the *Finin* and the *Shamrock*, both with Kelvic engines (petrol and paraffin) and fished lobster and mackerel in winter for export to the UK during the war. Sold from Crookhaven to Baltimore and then to the UK. The Hayes family of Long Island owned the *St Anne*, who fished out of Crookhaven.

1957 Denis O'Sullivan of Colla, Schull, got a new boat, the *Beal Ard*, fishing lobster out of Crookhaven. The Oulhen family, who were directors of the lobster ponds, brought over three boats from Brittany: the *Esperance*, the *Ariel* and the *Fleur de France*, which Dan O'Leary renamed *St Ita*.

1958 The Oulhens also bought the *Linnet*, which was skippered by Dan O'Leary.

1960 The *Britannia* was purchased in Mayo by Sean Flynn and Tim Coughlan, Goleen.

1966 Dan O'Leary bought the *Ros Glas*, which was subsequently lost in a storm in September 1983 in Goleen bay.

1968 A boat, *Lucky Me*, came from Cornwall with two English fishermen and had a very successful season fishing lobster.

1970 The *Ocean Spray* was built by Skinners in Baltimore and fished by John Goggin and Bill O'Mahony. It was taken over by Bill's nephews Jerry and Willie O'Mahony around 1990.

1972 Denis O'Sullivan bought the *Fastnet Fisher*, which was built in Bere Island by the Murphys.

1980 Jimmy Newman had a boat built by Paddy Hegarty, Oldcourt.

1987−97 Jimmy Newman had the *May Queen*.

1997 Jimmy Newman had the *Deirdre Karen*.

2002 Jimmy Newman had the second *Deirdre Karen*.

1981 Paul Bevkenkamp had a Dutch fishing boat, the *Leda*, used mostly for sea angling.

1995−2002 Tommy Flynn had the *Amber*.

1987−2007 Richard Notter owns the *Mary Helen*.

1995−2002 Richard Notter had the *Brid Marie*.

View of Lighthouse, Crookhaven.

LOWERTOWN AND SURROUNDING AREA

by Nellie O'Sullivan

The main settlement of Lowertown developed along the main road where the townland of Lowertown borders Arderavinna. This was the area chosen for Lowertown National School. Unfortunately it closed in 1971, even though the number of pupils on the roll was over 40. It was government policy at the time to close one- and two-teacher schools when the teachers retired or moved. This policy was changed very quickly.

The earliest dwelling houses here were the Twohig and McLean homes. Mrs McLean had a small shop and post office. Her only son, Michael, became involved in the struggle for freedom. He was shot by the British forces at Gaggin on 8th December 1920, aged eighteen years. The marble statue of Our Lady marks the place of his birth. It was the beginning of the end for his widowed mother, as she died with a broken heart within a year.

Michael O'Callaghan built his house and shop on the opposite side of the road where he also carried on his trade as a shoemaker. Patrick Hegarty, a blacksmith, built his forge where he shod many a horse and repaired farm machinery and carts. Last year the Lowertown Development Association built a replica village embodying the Post Office, the Forge and the dance platform. The platform was the centre of the social gatherings, especially on Sunday evenings.

As one walks along the by-road from Lowertown Church towards the coast road, one passes the old school residence. This was occupied by Master Hegarty and his family in the old days. Some of his family were also involved in the struggle for freedom and involved in the setting up of our State. Next we see the signal tower in Knock. As one continues to Ceann Conn, this magnificent view opens out before us, one of God's own masterpieces. We see from the islands to Gunpoint, to Castlepoint with its medieval O'Mahony castle to Crookhaven and beyond. There is a *cill* – a disused burial ground – in south Lowertown. It is overgrown now in the middle of a fine field. It is circular in shape. Upstanding headstones can still be seen and there is a souterrain or cavity in the middle. It is marked by one whitethorn tree. Coffinless corpses were brought here in Famine times in wheelbarrows or on back. Children were also buried there. The last person who was buried here was Mary Lucey, Balteen, in the mid-1900s.

There is an old ring fort two fields north east of the cill. There is a moat right around it and it's surrounded by sally trees. Both owners have respected these sites. The following are some of the numbers from the Lowertown National School roll call in bygone days: 1847 – 193 pupils; 1848 – 224 pupils; 1849 – 75 pupils. This is some of the history of Lowertown and surrounding areas.

Article from *Examiner*, Thursday 30th December 1965

A proposed design for a new church at Ballinskea, in the parish of Goleen, County Cork, has been prepared. The new church, when built, will replace the 138-year-old existing structure which is in poor condition. Repairs would be so extensive that it was decided by his Lordship the Bishop of Cork and Ross, Most Rev Dr Lucey, to go ahead with plans to build a new church.

In the old church, Mass was celebrated only on Sundays and there was no reservation of the Blessed Sacrament. To achieve this it will be necessary to build a priest's residence beside the church. The cost of the proposed scheme will be between 35,000 and 40,000.

An appeal to past and present parishioners has been launched to finance the building of the new church.

Pictures (top) show the old church and the proposed new building.

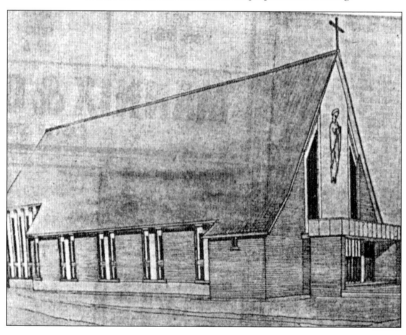

This photo taken from Mount Gabriel is taking view of a very big portion of Goleen Parish.

The Community Council before entering their new complex for one of their monthly meetings, included are Michael Collins, Joe Hurley, Denis Downey, Paul O'Sullivan, Pat McCarthy, Denis O'Neill, Anthony O'Callaghan, Vickie Evans, Tommy Gerymen, Maureen Newman, Ellen Scully and Timmie Barnett.

'Many hands make light work'. Photo of ticket sellers who travelled troughout West Cork to sell tickets for the 'Community Field' draw.

Mr. John O'Donoghue, Minister for Sport and Tourism with Denis O'Donovan T.D. and members of Goleen Community Council to discuss funding for the Community Field. Included are Paul O'Sullivan Chairman, Connie O'Driscoll, Eamonn Sheehan, Ellen Scully, Denis Downey, Joe Hurley, also in the photo Pat McCarthy and Connie Bowen.

The Goleen Community Council 2004–2007. Front row, from left to right: Geraldine Camier (secretary), Joe Hurley, Denis Downey, Paul O'Sullivan (chairman), Ellen Scully (treasuer), Vickie Evans. Back row: Sue Hill, Michael Collins, Denis O'Neill, Anthony O'Callaghan, Timmie Barnett, Pat McCarthy, Connie O'Driscoll. Missing from the photo: Maureen Newman, Eamonnn Sheehan and Tommy Gerymen.

South West Junior semi-final 2007, between Muintir Bhaire and Caheragh. Showing the Sports Complex and view of spectators.

'Ready to Roll'. After three months travelling the highways and by-ways from Dursey Island to Kinsale selling tickets for the £10,000 draw, the drum is ready to roll, watched by Community Council members Connie O'Driscoll, Paul O'Sullivan, Eamonn Sheehan, Maurice Coughlan, Maureen Newman, Denis Downey, Anthony O'Callaghan, Geraldine Camier, Ellen Scully, Joe Hurley, Tommy Jerymen, Sue Hill and Michael Collins.

Some of the past pupils of the old 'Lissigriffin School' seen here at the unveiling of the plaque to mark the site on 29th July 2006.

All-Ireland half set winners 2006, pictured with Anne Murray, National President of ICA.
Dancers: Emily Nolan, Breda Buckley, Liz Barry and Genevieve Tuit.

Field Committee members with Denis O'Donovan, TD, and Paddy Sheehan, MCC, look-
ing over the community field in its early sages of reclamation included are Paul O'Sullivan,
Connie O'Driscoll, Maurice Coughlan, Denny O'Donoghue, Denis Downey, Anthony
O'Callaghan, Eamonn Sheehan, Timmie Barnett and Joe Hurley.

Goleen Junior Championship Team 2006

Back, from left: Aron Lucey, Derek Barnett, Tim Murnane, Jason Nyhan, Joe Mahoney, Richard Cotter, David O'Leary, Kevin Kennedy, Liam Donovan and Declan Hodnett. Front, from left: Liam Connell, Patrick Scully, David Barry, Brendan Scully, Danny Driscoll, Edward Burchill, Keiran Sheehan, John Cullinane, Daniel Driscoll, William Burchill, Brendan O'Regan and Pat Kennedy.

Goleen National School 2006. Front row, from left: David Franzoni, Danny Cullinane, Rowan Flatman, Kellie McGirr, Jean-Paul V/D Vlugt, Jodie Connell, Nicole Whooley. Second row, from left: Gerald Downing, Robert Franzoni, Mark O'Reilly, Inez Connell, Cliodhna Cullinane, Tadhg Cullinane, Michelle Murnane, Brid Kennedy, Chris-Sophie V/D Vlugt, Clodagh Hellen, Debbie Walsh, Miss O'Shea, Mrs Lannin. Third row, from left: Miss Crowley, Bryony Flatman, David Hodnett, Tomas Harrington, Cathal O'Sullivan, Brendan Goggin, Daryl Connell, David Donovan, Niamh Whooley, Lisa O'Driscoll. Fourth row, from left: Sean Sheehan, Orla Donovan, Paudie Scully, Aran Barry, Aimee Greenway, Ronan Kennedy, Michael Goggin, Sean Lucey, Jessie Flatman, Katie Scully.

At the unveiling of the plaque to mark the site of the old Lissigriffin N.S. on July 2006 by one of its past pupils Sr. Veronica. Included are Fr. O'Donovan, Rev. Ethna Lynch, Sr. Veronica and past pupils Denis Downey and Joe Hurley who got the plaque erected.

'Showing the strain in 2005'. Tug-of-war at Goleen Festival.

Lissigriffin NS. Front row, from left: Niall O'Driscoll, Kieran O'Driscoll, Marie Sheehan, Caoimhe Reidy, Mia Kelly, Sam Coughlan, John Supple, James Kelly, Ellen O'Driscoll, Katie O'Sullivan. Second row, from left: Eimear Sheehan, Ciara Sheehan, Padraig Downey, Jed Little, Megan Costello, Padraig Reidy, James O'Driscoll, Catherine Sheehan, Ashling O'Driscoll, Michelle O'Leary, Laoise O'Driscoll, Mairead Supple, Eoghan Sheehan, Katie Downey. Third row, from left: Lily Little, Roisin Reidy, Siobhan O'Driscoll, Heather O'Leary, Miss Griffin, Mr Lannin, Sinead Supple, Shane O'Leary.

They may have their jaunting cars in Killarney but here in Goleen well-known jarvey Noel O'Donovan is awaiting to take visitors around Goleen's beauty spots.

Crookhaven

I was born near lovely Crookhaven,
Where the soft south west breezes do blow,
Where the Mizen Head lights the dark evening.
That the ships a safe journey will go.
As a boy I played around Rock Street,
'Marconi' came down the same road,
To send out the world's first message,
It was known at the time as 'Morse Code'.

But hard times sent me off from my homeland,
I took a last glimpse of the brow,
As I circled around past Rock Island,
And Goleen ahead of me now.
My heart it was sore, yes, and sorry,
To be leaving that wonderful scene,
The swans on the lake gliding peaceful,
the Sands, too, and over Balteen.

I have travelled the wide world over,
And I've seen the great rat race of man,
50 years far away – from the old haunts,
I could never forget its life span.
I oft dreamt as I slept here in exile,
Of the fun and the sport – that had been,
The crowds around the pier in the summer,
And the days that I played with Goleen.

Now I thank the Great Lord in His wisdom,
That He steered me right back home again,
To see my old school Lissigriffin,
Where I mixed with the greatest of men.
I have met just a few, the rest have passed on,
Away up through Heaven's great door,
And next time I'll leave you, Crookhaven,
I'll be laid with my friends in Kilmoe.

GOLEEN ICA

by Breda Buckley

The ICA was founded in Co Wexford in May 1910. The aim at that time was to better the standard of life's opportunities for women, their families and their communities in rural Ireland. Since its foundation, the Association has made an immense contribution to both the rural and urban life of the nation, through its organised structure of county federations and local guilds involving women of every age and from all walks of life. They have lobbied, supported and encouraged government bodies on many issues and have been instrumental in the introduction of various schemes down through the decades. The regular guild meeting, whether in a remote village, small town or city, enriches the lives of its members, develops dormant talents, enabling members to learn new skills, to relax, to entertain and be entertained, offering friendship, support, good relationships, good neighbourliness and, in general, makes life happier.

Cork Federation held their inaugural meeting in the Town Hall, Bandon, on 25th January 1936 with seven guilds present. It has come a long way since then, presently there are 95 guilds with over 2,000 members in Cork Federation.

Schull, Goleen and Ballydehob Guild was set up in November 1965. Over the years the guild campaigned successfully for improvements both locally and nationally. Ballydehob moved on and formed their own guild in March 1980. The support from Goleen ladies for the Schull/Goleen Guild continued and was evident. The participated in all activities and events, and there was great joy in Goleen when, in 1988, the guild won the Patsy Lawlor all-Ireland ½ set competition, as two of the participants were local – Liz Barry and Breda Buckley. Many of the guild's presidents were from Goleen.

In 2001 the Goleen girls felt they were ready to build their own guild. The first meeting was held on 9th May 2001 in the Parish Hall. Judy Murphy was elected president, Angela Stafford, vice-president, Breda Buckley, secretary, Noreen Hurley, treasurer, and Winnie

O'Brien, PRO. There were 54 members that first year. We celebrated our inaugurations with a very successful concert. We were charmed to have international soprano Mary Hegarty as our guest and she was supported by local artists. Goleen has an inclusive and active guild with a wealth of talent, which has gone from strength to strength over the past six years, representing all facets of our community. From September to May, guild meetings are held on the second Wednesday of each month in the Parish Hall at 8.30pm. These are lively and informative with various guest speakers who address a wide range of topics. Members are always interested in developing their talents, adding new expertise and getting involved in ICA current events and competitions. The parish can be proud of the guild and its achievements. Member have competed with the best and brought the honours back to Goleen. Members have excelled in competition at West Cork and county level. These include: art, baking, crafts, charades, decoupage, healthy eating, recycling, quiz, variety show, drama, essay writing, group ballad singing, solo singing, solo, 2-hand, ½ set and set dancing, poetry, monologue, story composition and telling in both Irish and English. But the jewel in the crown must surely be winning two all-Ireland finals. In 2006 the Patsy Lawlor all-Ireland ½ set competition was won by Liz Barry, Breda Buckley, Emily Nolan and Genevieve Tuit. The guild also represented Cork Federation in the full set competition – included were the four ladies already mentioned, joined by Catherine McCarthy, Noelle Roycroft, Mary Coughlan and Nuala O'Brien. In 2004 Catherine O'Driscoll won the National Photographic Competition. In 2003 our dancers were runners-up in the all-Ireland ½ set competition – they were Liz Barry, Breda Buckley, Jean Collins and Winnie O'Brien. These were joined by Joan Notter, Noelle Roycroft, Josephine Hegarty and Olive Lynch to represent Cork Federation in the full set competition. Betty Johnson also represented Cork Federation in the solo singing competition that year.

The younger generation has not been forgotten. Mothers encourage their children to participate in the children's competitions of arts, story and essay writing, and we have had winners in each section.

The guild won the 'Endeavour Award' in 2004 and 2005. This trophy is awarded to the guild with most involvement in ICA affairs within Cork Federation. A great achievement for the guild furthest away from the city. We also won the 'West Cork Guild of the Year' in 2005.

On a more serious note, when South Doc was introduced to West Cork, the guild voiced their concerns regarding its function in such a rural area. The guild made a submission to the Department of Justice, Equality and Law Reform on the Draft National Plan for Women. This can be viewed on the department's website. We organised an open meeting and welcomed speakers from the Marie Keating Foundation to advise on cancer information and awareness.

Each year we hold a fundraising event and there has been great support for charitable causes. To date, we have made contributions to Schull Hospital (annually), New York Firefighters (9/11), Tsunami Asian Fund, RNLI, Cork ARC Cancer Support, Headways Ireland, Cystic Fibrosis, MS, Rehab, Bantry Cope Foundation and the Good Shepherd Services, Cork.

The guild was honoured to host the social to celebrate the 150th anniversary of St Patrick's Cathedral Church and the social evening on the occasion of Fr McLaughlin's departure; both evenings were held in the Parish Hall and were very successful.

An Grianán is the ICA's Adult Education College, situated near the long, sandy beaches of Co Louth. It is open all year round for weekend, weekly and daily courses. It is built on a 78-acre site with spacious gardens, lovely walks and a high standard of accommodation. A perfect venue to revitalise oneself. Each year some of our members attend this idyllic haven and combine enhancing their skills with a social occasion. New friendships are formed as guilds from other counties are also present.

The guild has an end-of-year outing in May and a dinner dance in November. Both are great fun and occasions not to be missed.

The ICA is a vibrant and vital part of Irish life. For almost 100 years, guilds up and down the country have provided a welcome to the stranger, solace to the lonely and the hand of friendship to women of all persuasions. There is always a very warm welcome to new members who wish to join this valuable organisation.

AN GARDA SÍOCHÁNA

by Michael O'Reilly

An Garda Síochána was founded in 1922. The first garda arrived in Goleen in 1923. The first station occupied by the gardaí in Goleen was the present post office. A new garda station, still in use, was built in 1928. General Eoin O'Duffy, the Commissioner of An Garda Síochána, visited the new station on 30th April 1929. The station consisted of a public office, sergeants office, one bedroom, a cell and a kitchen.

Married quarters for sergeant and family was attached to the station proper. Heating was solid fuel in two fireplaces. There was no water supply to the station and the toilet facilities were 'Elsan' dry toilets. Public water supply was connected to the station in 1961. Flushed toilets were installed in 1969. The ESB was connected to the station in 1960. The Office of Public Works was responsible for the building and upkeep of the station. It was redecorated every five years internally, and every seven years externally. Telephone communication was by way of dialling Goleen Post Office Exchange where courtesy of the post master, the late Mr Jack Harrington (RIP), the call was put through the Goleen Exchange for local calls, or through Skibbereen Exchange for outside calls. This service was available up to 10pm, after which time the Garda Station phone was connected to the Skibbereen Exchange. Goleen Garda Station phone number was Goleen 2. After 10pm, Goleen Garda Station was on a 'party' line and so shared a direct line to the Skibbereen Exchange. Two rings on the phone was the system for contacting Goleen Garda Station after 10pm. The system was in operation up to 1st April 1978.

From their arrival in Goleen, the Gardaí were occupied with the enforcement of the law as it related to the Goleen area. The Road Traffic Act was breached on occasions by 'wandering' animals and unlit bicycles; motor vehicles were scarce and so did not feature in too many prosecutions. Liquor Licensing Laws were lenient by enforcement, as the importance of their role in the social life of the community was understood and appreciated. The Noxious Weeds Act (thistle, dock, ragwort) breaches thereof, were dealt with mostly by way of a warning notice to destroy the offending weeds.

The enforcement of the Dogs Act (unlicensed dogs) usually resulted in a rush to the post office to have the offending canines licensed, another small boost to the coffers of the State. The supervision of the expenditure of the explosives in rock blasting for land reclamation purposes through the 1960s was the duty of the Gardaí.

All these duties and patrols were carried out by the Gardaí, either walking or on bicycles.

During the war years, 1939 to 1945, and for a few years before and after, 'wrack' featured prominently in the lives of people living around the coast of Ireland, and the Goleen coast was no different. The Gardaí at Goleen were the receivers of wreck for the area, and all wreck found or taken was required by law to be exported by the finders to the Gardaí. Barrels of whiskey and rum, said to be in excess of 100%, were cause for great local entertainment, as the 'wrack' takers sought to outwit the Gardaí, whose job it was to seize and confiscate all liquor so obtained. Little attention seems to have been paid to other forms of 'wrack'.

Local and general elections required the Gardaí to supervise the polling stations at Crookhaven NS, Lissigriffin NS, Goleen NS and Dunmanus NS, and at the close of poll, to escort the ballot boxes to Schull Garda Station for transfer to the court centre at Clonakilty. The enforcement of the School Attendance Acts was the job of a garda, appointed school attendant officer for Goleen Garda Station area.

Hereunder is a list of sergeants and gardaí attached to Goleen Garda Station from 1955. Earlier records are not available.

1955–6	Sgt Hayden, gardaí Luddy and Cassidy
1956–7	Sgt Downing, gardaí Luddy and Cassidy
1957–9	Sgt Noone, gardaí Luddy and Cassidy
1959	Sgt Jennings, gardaí Costello and Cassidy
1959	Sgt Hogan, gardaí Healy and Murphy
1959–61	Sgt Sloyan, gardaí Healy and Ryan
1961–7	Garda John Breen
1967–96	Garda Michael O'Reilly
1996	Gardaí Dan Harrington and Anthony Finn

GOLEEN GAA CLUB

by Eamonn Sheehan

Goleen GAA Club was formed in 1956. Previous to that any footballers from the parish played with Schull or Bantry. It was suggested at the Muintir na Tire meeting that a GAA club be formed in the parish. Father John O'Mahony was its first chairman. Bart O'Meara, NT, secretary and treasurer; Peter O'Neill, Sean Hegarty and Bart O'Meara, selectors. It was decided to enter a team in the junior 2 championship and Denis O'Meara was elected captain.

The first two years brought little success, but in 1959 the club won the South West junior 'B' football championship against Newcestown on a very wet day, and the score line was 3-0 to 1-4. Goleen then played junior 'A' football in 1960 and, for the next four years, were a match good enough for all the junior 'A' teams in West Cork. They won the junior 'A' league in 1962 and contested the championship 'B' final against Barryroe in 1964, losing by two points. After the loss of players due to emigration, the club went out of existence in 1966.

During the short and successful period of the club, Diarmuid O'Sullivan was captain of the team in 1959 and 1960, and was also the Carbery senior full back. Danny O'Driscoll also played in goal for Carbery. Jim Buckley was captain in 1961; Billy O'Sullivan in 1963; Denis Downey in 1964. In 1963, Denis Harrington won an All-Ireland Championship Hurling medal with Farranferris. In 1969, the late Donal Collins also won an All-Ireland Championship Hurling medal with Farranferris.

The Goleen GAA Club was reformed again in 1979. Previous to that, we had been kicking ball around the sandbanks for fun. A group got together in early 1979 and we had our first game against St Gabriel's on St Patrick's Day, which we won by one point. We had Danny O'Driscoll playing in goal again, as he did in the early 1960s, so providing a link between the old team and the new, after 13 years. Dermot Sheehan was first secretary, and Father O'Connor was first chairman.

In the early 1980s, the junior team was successful to the point that it reached the under-21 final with Kilmeen, to be beaten by same, as they beat us also in the junior 'B' championship. The same year we were hit with emigration in the early 1980s, so our numbers were limited but, nevertheless, we kept going, also reaching the 'B' final in 1987, but losing.

Our underage players started with Muintir Bhaire in the early 1980s, as we had no underage club, and then joined with Gabriel Rangers in 1984 to form Gabriel Óg, winning the county in 1986 in under-16 football, and reaching the Rural final in 1987, but losing same to Ballinora. Then, in 1988, they won the minor county. There were several players from the Goleen parish playing on the Gabriel Óg team, namely: John Cullinane, Tim Donovan, Kieran Sheehan, Patrick Downey and Martin Walsh.

Goleen GAA Club then started their own underage club in 1992, namely Mizen Rovers, in under-12, under-14 and under-16 football only. The first officers of this club were Vincie Goggin, chairman; Kieran Sheehan, secretary; Richie Barry, treasurer; Joe O'Sullivan, vice-chairman. The Goleen club entered Scór na nÓg in 1985 with a lot of success at Carbery, and some in the county. We had a ballad group, who went to the county final in 1988, namely Ciara Buckley, Bernie Coughlan, Mary Downey, Ann Downey and Isabella Hodnett. In 1991 Seamus Downey won a Carbery final for recitation. The ballad group of Ciara Buckley, Tara O'Sullivan, Isabella Hodnett and Bernadette Hodnett won again in 1993 in the Carbery final, and, in 1995, Sharon Buckley won for solo singing.

In 1993 we also entered Scór na Páistí, which was formed for national schools only, and we also entered Scór Sinsear in 1996. Marion Donovan went to the county final in Scór na Páistí in 1994 for recitation. The ballad group of Geni Tuite, Tara O'Sullivan, Isabella Hodnett, Bernadette Hodnett and Mary Downey went to the county final in Scór Sinsear in 1996. David Barry won Carbery Scór na nÓg for recititation in 1996. Scór lapsed in the late 1990s, but it is activated again and Scór na Páistí is entered once more, plus Scór Sinsear since 2006.

Since 1988 on the playing field we were getting results but not to finals until 1993 when we got to the junior league final against St Colum's in Bantry, winning by two points. Our underage was starting to pay dividends, as this team was very young. We also went to the junior 'B' championship final in 1995 against Diarmuid Ó Mathúna's. We lost by four points and we also lost a league final to Kilmac in 1995.

In 1999 we won the under-21 football championship in Skibbereen; what an occasion, with Michael Burchill as captain. Sadly, that quiet man has passed away from us – *Ar dheis De go raibh anam dilis.* (We won't see his likes again.)

On 10th November 1996 we won the junior 'C' championship, captained by Donal O'Driscoll. We qualified for this by being knocked out in the first round of the junior 'B' championship. We were competing with junior 1 second teams. We beat St James', who were also 'B' grade, Ballinascarthy's second team, and we beat Newcestown in the final by a point. This Newcestown team would have been equivalent to junior 1 because their first team were Intermediate. We also lost the league final on 30th November 1996, to St Colum's.

We held the South West GAA convention in Goleen Hall in 1995 and we will be holding it again this year, 2007, in the new community complex. Through the late 1990s, John Cullinane and Finbarr Downey have played senior football with Carbery, as has Finbarr's brother Seamus played senior football with UCC, winning a county final in 1999. John Notter also won an All-Ireland senior 'B' football championship with Farranferris in 1983.

Up until 2002 all our players were training and playing in Duach. We weren't allowed to improve this pitch, so we got a loan of a field from Richard O'Connell, until 2005; the Community Field was then ready and is now our home. We had various small venues for training, namely Alex Hamilton, Sue Hills and parish properties over the years since the early 1980s. We have various players in our midst; for example, we had two Germans who started at underage with us in 1993 – Moritz and Philip Eder. Philip went on to win a Carbery under-21 medal in our winning year of 1999. They have moved back to Germany – our loss – and a lot of that team have emigrated also. Today we have junior 'B', under-21 and Minor football, but the underage has blossomed. We now have under-10, under-12, under-14 and under-16 in both hurling and football, with summer camps now the norm. It is great to see youngsters taking an interest. The trojan work done by the mentors, namely Timmy Sheehan (Letter), Pat and Derry Kennedy, Paul Sullivan and Bernie Falvey from Antrim, who played camogie for same.

We have had various trainers over the years from within the club and from outside. Trainers in the early 1980s were: Jim Currig from Schull, Seamus Davis from Lisheen and Ollie Collins from Balteen. Then, in the 1990s, we had Patrick Hodnett from Ballydehob, Eamonn Sheehan from Goleen, Steven Dineen from Bantry Blues, who transferred to us in the late 1990s, and Terry Minehane from Skibbereen, and this year we have gone home-based with Kieran Sheehan and Timmy Sheehan helping due to him looking after Minors.

Goleen SW Cork Junior 2 football champions 1959. Back row: B O'Meara, D O'Meara, D Downey, D Cotter, P O'Neill, D Sullivan, J Buckley, J O'Connor, J Sheehan, D Donovan, F Arundel, D O'Driscoll, R Sugrue, D Coughlan, J Moynihane. Front row: M Sullivan, S Harrington, B Sullivan, D Sullivan (captain), P Coughlan, J Downey, J Lyons, T McSweeney.

Chairmen have been Fr O'Connor, Fr Murphy, and Dermot Sheehan from 1979 to 1995; Donal O'Sullivan, Dunmanus, and Tim Sheehan, Colleras, in 2000; and Eamon Sheehan from 2002 to 2007. Secretaries: Dermot Sheehan 1979 to 1983; Tim Cullinane from 1983 to 1984; Tim Sheehan in 1984; Kieran O'Sullivan from 1988 to 1991; Eamonn Sheehan from 1992 to 1998; Paul O'Sullivan from 1998 to 2002; and Donal O'Driscoll from 2002 to 2006. Junior captains same as above.

The infrastructure of the club is very young. Hopefully it will stay in existence, as it is under pressure from emigration – five juniors have emigrated in 2007. Let's hope the GAA will go from strength to strength with our new state-of-the-art facilites.

The following article appeared in *The Southern Star*, 12th December 1959:

'Goleen win South West title'

Goleen 3-0; Newcestown 1-4
Goleen became South West Cork junior 2 football champions on Sunday at Rossa Park, when they defeated Newcestown. The game, played in drenching rain, which made things unpleasant for the players and good attendance, was keenly contested and the excitement was intense, particularly in the closing stages. Great credit is due to both victors and vanquished for the fine football fare served up on such a dismal afternoon. Goleen were worthy winners after a stern struggle, but no one can deny that Newcestown had more than their fair share of bad luck, particularly in the scoring line. Still victory invariably comes to the team that takes its chances and Goleen were not remiss in this respect.

Newcestown lead

Newcestown attacked almost incessantly. In the first half their approach being first class but many good chances went a-begging. This, in many cases, was due to the slippery ball, but over-anxiety was a contributory cause. Their tally in this period was three points to no score for Goleen, which was hardly an inadequate return for the continuous pressure exerted by the losers.

How meagre it was became clear on the resumption when Sean Harrington took full advantage with as nice a goal as one could wish to see. He followed a fast ball past a defence caught flatfooted and booted the leather out of the goalkeeper's reach with a very deft kick. The cheering had hardly died when the same player tricked the backs again and slammed the ball to the net for the lead for Goleen.

These scores should almost inevitably have been the signal for a Newcestown collapse, but they recovered and gave as good as they got for the remainder of the game. After some ten minutes, they added a point, but again Goleen came back for a well-taken goal which seemed to put the issue beyond doubt. But it was only then that we saw the real thrills.

Newcestown came back, mounted attack after attack, and five minutes from time a fine goal put them but two points behind, but that was as close as they got. At this stage, the Goleen rearguard really rose to occasion, as many another defence would have cracked under the strain in the dying minutes. However, no praise is too great for the losers, who kept trying to the end. As footballers, they had more finesse all round than Goleen, but brilliant individual efforts by Goleen more than offset the advantage. Goleen's trump card was, however, their ability to adapt themselves to the atrocious weather conditions of Sunday.

For his brilliant goals, Harrington must get pride of place on the Goleen team, but the Herculean work of Buckley, Sullivan, Sugrue and McSweeney deserves mention, as while they were maybe less spectacular, they were no less effective in their contribution to victory. For Newcestown, N Kiely was a very useful forward and took his scores well while S Collins in the centre and Dineen and Allen in defence were the pick of a fast clever combination.

Finally, a word of praise to all thirty men who diplayed amazing stamina and no little football ability on one of the wettest and most unpleasant days for a long time. K McCarthy (Rossas) was an impartial and competent referee.

Goleen team: D O'Driscoll, J Downey, D O'Sullivan, M O'Sullivan, F Arundel, T McSweeney, D O'Donovan, J Buckley, M Riordan, J Lyons, D Cotter, D O'Meara, P Coughlan, R Sugrue, S Harrington.

Dhurode's Fair Hills and Valleys

Dhurode's fair hills and valleys,
Are the fairest that I know;
Like sparkling gems of silver,
And shining lumps of gold.
The stone crushers and water wheels,
And fine machinery,
Are all in charge of old Pad Long,
From the English Company.

They were erected by McCormick
From the heart of Goleen town,
He drained this lovely valley,
Forced the water up and down
And he built that great hydraulic
To make the big wheels go
'Un biaste fein,' said old Pad Long,
'I see tons of copper ore.'

'My boys, throw away your cibbles
Let them in the drivins lay
And we'll put water whistling
Down through Dunmanus bay.'
And to sit above this valley
On a dark and dreamy night,
You'd think it was a city
Lit by electric light.

And if you search this wide world o'er
No happier lads you'll see,
Than Con Coughlan and Dan Reilly
And the three sons with Curly
And as they walk a shady grove
The pretty girls to see
They are happier than the Prince of Wales
Who rides in his buggy.

And now once more I'm landed here
But I'm sorry to have to say
The valley it is darkened
And the miners gone away.
The shores are dim, the hills look grim
And I heard poor Richard say,
There are tons of gold and silver
At the bottom of the bay.

Crookhaven 1930s

PARISH ARCHAEOLOGICAL AND HISTORIC SITES

by Denis Downey

In recent years, the end of the roadway at Mizen Head has become a popular starting or finishing point for different individuals or groups raising money for some very worthy causes. It has seen walkers, cyclists, runners, horses and traps, horse back riders, vintage tractors, vintage cars and even a pram pusher starting or finishing there to or from various parts of the country.

On 25th June 2005 a plaque was veiled there in memory of all the people who worked at the building of the Fastnet Rock Lighthouse 100 years earlier, and it has the following inscription:

> 'A replica of the twentieth course of the granite built Fastnet Rock Lighthouse reduced to half size, has been laid out here in order to mark the centenary of the first exhibition of its light on the 27th June 1904.
>
> 'The two granite seats are full-size examples of some of the interlocking stones used in its construction. The tower was designed by Mr William Douglas, engineer to the Commissioners of Irish Lights, and built under the direction of Mr CV Scott and Mr James Kavanagh, who set every stone of the tower between 1896 and 1903.
>
> 'In memory of those who built this masterpiece of lighthouse engineering for the safety of all mariners.'

This plaque was unveiled by the chairman of the Commissioners of Irish Lights, Mr JF Boland. On a noticeboard nearby, the following information is shown:

The Fasnet Lighthouse Century Stone Course

Just over 100 years later, on 25th June 2005, the chairman of the Commissioners of Irish Lights, Mr Frank Boland, marked the century of the event by unveiling the half-sized granite replicas of the actual stone blocks, which weigh almost 3 tonnes each. This memorial is laid out in commemoration of all those people who manned and maintained it so well in its first 100 years of existence.

The construction of the lighthouse was an undertaking of enormous complexity for the period in which it was built. A total of 2,074 granite blocks, weighing 4,300 tonnes were cut to precise specification at Penwryn in Cornwall and transported to Rock Island in Crookhaven from where a specifically built steamship, the SS *Ierne*, brought them out to the rock.

Signal towers

The parish has the distinction of having three signal towers: Leamcon, Brow Head and Cloughane. These were part of the coastal defence system built when a French invasion seemed imminent. From each tower you could view another one on either side. From Leamcon you could see Brow Head, 8 miles to the west. From Brow Head you can see the Cloughane signal tower 3 miles to the west, which communicated with the tower at Sheep's Head, some 6 miles to the north.

Work on the three signal towers started in 1804, which were completed and weather slated a year later; then the signal masts were erected. Signal lieutenants were appointed to Cloughane in October 1804 and Leamcon and the Brow Head in September 1805. The 200th anniversary of the towers was celebrated by lighting fires at each tower at 3 p.m. on a Sunday evening, 19th August. This is a short history of the signal towers.

Mass rocks

Balteen, Colleras-Oughter, Lowertown.

Promontory fort

Dunkelly East. It is thought that a castle of the O'Mahoneys' once stood in the area, but it cannot be positively identified. The promontory fort on the coast is of course invincible.

Holy wells

Letter, Colleras-Oughter, Dunlough, Castlepoint, Cashelfean, Kilbrown.

Arderawinney wedge tomb

Situated on the north side of the main road from Schull and about half a mile before Altar.

Lissacaha ring fort

A particularly notable triple-fossed ring fort with very tall banks and mound-like constructions within the enclosure. Known as the 'Fort of the Battle', but not known why, it is a massive fort that evokes all the wonder of these ancient places.

Castlepoint Leamcon Castle

Standing on its precarious headland and yet surviving all the torments of the Atlantic weather, this O'Mahony Castle is said to have been the last to surrender after the English invasion at the beginning of the 7th century. Also known as 'Black Castle', it is superbly constructed and fairly well looked after.

Mines

The following is a list of the townlands where copper mines can be found: Ballysallagh, Kilbarry, Castlepoint, Cloghane, Dubhrode, Mallavogue, Dunmanus West, Derryleary, Balteen (East). Derryfunction where brytes can be found.

Lissagriffin early church

Kilmoe Church is said to be eleventh or twelfth century, and is important for its Hiberno-Romanesque-style altar window. Few examples exist in Ireland and it is good to know that restoration work has been finally undertaken to preserve the gable wall of the church.

Altar wedge tombs

To date, three wedge tombs have been discovered around this inlet, two of which have recently been excavated and reconstructed. One is by the road just after it turns right after Arderawinney and the other is directly behind the Altar restaurant. The finds from these sites are extremely important and help to establish the date of these, the region's earliest megalithic monuments.

Arduslough wedge tombs and carved stone

A bit of effort is required to locate the sites in the area around Arduslough. At least three wedge tombs, two of which are in good state of preservation, are virtually camouflaged in the hillsides and the remains of a collapsed one stands on the hilltop. East of the lake, just as the road descends, is another lake near which is the wonderfully carved stone of Castlemehigan. This ancient stones is said to mark the site of an early monastic settlement and among the large disc-shaped carvings, a cross has been inscribed.

Mizen Peak cairns

The curiously conical last hill of Ireland at the end of the Mizen owes its pronounced shape to the fact that it was crowned in prehistoric times with a cairn. Other cairns can also be found on its slopes.

Kilcomane old church

The ruins here are of an ancient church that was dedicated to St Daman.

Fish palaces

Ballynaule, Leenane, Drishane.

Dunmanus cromlechs

In the marshes in the inner part of the bay are two boulder dolmens which now stand right on the high-water mark and are sometimes submerged. One is easy enough to locate and a second lies half buried nearby. A third existed near a nearby cottage which burnt down shortly after its removal by the owner.

Fulachta fiadh

Derryfunction, Greenane, Cloughanekilleen, Letter, Lisacha, Rathooragh, Colleras-Oughter.

Cills

Ballyrisode, Lowertown, Kilbarry, Cloughanekilleen, Killeane, Enoughter.

Lime kilns

Cove, Ballydevlin.

Wedge tombs

Ballydevlin, Ballyvogue-Beg, Ballyrisode.

Baulán stone

Lissigriffin, Toormore.

Forts

Cashelfean, Knockeens.

LIEUTENANT MICHAEL JOHN McLEAN

by John C O'Sullivan

Lieutenant Michael John McLean, Lowertown, Schull, a member of the West Cork Flying Column of the Irish Republican Army was killed at Cashelbeg, Gaggin, Bandon, on December 8, 1920. He was only 18 years of age. His father, John McLean, was a native of Foherla, Aughadown, Skibbereen. His mother was Kate McLean, the local postmistress, who also had a grocery shop and farm at Lowertown. She was formerly Sexton, with brothers James and Michael, living at Foherla, Aughadown, Skibbereen, and sisters Mrs Walsh, residing at Ardralla, Mrs Hegarty, Lissacaha, Schull, and Mrs Lehane, Lissigriffin, Goleen. Mary Ellen, the firstborn child of John and Kate McLean, was two years older than Michael John, who was born on 5th March 1902 and baptised on 7th March 1902 at the Church of St Patrick, Goleen, by Rev J O'Sullivan, CC, the sponsors being Mary Lehane and James Sexton. Both children attended Lowertown NS and when their school days were over, they helped at home.

The 1916 Rising, the execution of its leaders and the tragic events of later years, caused Michael John great distress. The death of James Connolly, who was crippled from wounds that he received in the Rising, and who was strapped to a wheelchair and shot, was in his view barbaric. In November 1920 he was incensed by the execution of Kevin Barry, also 18 years of age, and by the slaughter in Croke Park on Bloody Sunday. His father died on 30th November 1918 and, before that, Michael John had joined the Leamcon Company of the Irish Republican Army at Leamcon House, Schull, then owned by the Cowhig family and formerly owned by Mr Hull, a landlord. The captain of the company was Michael O'Donovan, Gunpoint, Schull. Michael John McLean was appointed a lieutenant. Later he attended a training camp at Dunmanus. Officers in charge of training were Gibbs Ross, Glandart, Bantry, and Sean Lehane of Scart, Bantry.

In November 1920, Michael John and three other officers were prepared for service with the Flying Column, an armed active service unit which was always on the move back and forth throughout West Cork. Selected to join the column with McLean were Lieutenant Con Sheehan of Glaun, Schull, who was a native of Cape Clear, Tom F O'Driscoll of Dunmanus, and Jack Collins of Dunkelly, Goleen. Michael McLean, who was then employed as a postman, arranged that Fianna Éireann member Christy Coughlan of Balteen, Schull, would replace him as postman. As a matter of interest, Christy, who later resided in London, addressed numerous Anti-Partition meetings in Hyde Park. It was arranged that Lieutenant McLean and comrades would leave for Kilmichael on 26th November 1920. The last person in the locality who saw Michael John was Volunteer Tim O'Mahony, Drinane, Schull, who gave McLean a haircut on the night before he left.

At dawn on the morning of 26th November, Michael John and his comrades set off for Kilmichael in a horse and trap, arriving on the 28th, but as the column were in ambush positions, they were placed behind the front line with orders to come forward and take over from wounded volunteers. When Lieutenant James O'Sullivan of Knockawaddra was wounded, Lieutenant Michael John McLean came forward to take his place. Lieutenant James O'Sullivan died, as also did Commandant Michael McCarthy, Dunmanway, and Lieutenant Pat Deasy, Bandon. The 18 British auxiliaries were wiped out. The men of the column captured their rifles, ammunition and papers. After the ambush it was a long march to Granure. Next day the column moved off. On 8th December it had reached Cashelbeg, Gaggin.

Lieutenant McLean, who fell into a drain and hurt his arm, was sent to a local farmhouse by Commandant Charlie Hurley, to warn the occupants to remain indoors until the signal for withdrawal was heard. The column took up ambush positions at two locations awaiting a lorry of Black and Tans coming from the Clonakilty direction. The orders given to the column were misunderstood with the result that the first group allowed the lorry to pass and the second column group fired only a few shots. The column withdrew. The lorry stopped some distance away. The Black and Tans came into the fields and McLean was captured. As they prepared to shoot him, the farmer objected. They dragged him down the narrow by-road at Cashelbeg, tortured him mercilessly and shot him. It is said that they tied him to a lorry and dragged him along the road. The scenes afterwards were very harrowing, especially the heart-rending cries of his widowed mother when she saw the condition of his body. It was the beginning of the end for her; she died on 23rd November 1921. She is buried in the Abbey, Skibbereen.

**Ned and Mary Ellen O'Sullivan (née McLean, Michael's sister) at the statue in
Lowertown, on 16th August 1959.**

The remains of Michael John now rest in the Republican Plot in
Bandon Church grounds, where also lie the remains of seven other
freedom fighters. The graves are marked individually by low uniform
headstones. These republicans are prayed for at masses in Bandon
and Gaggin every Easter Sunday.

Mary Ellen McLean married Captain Ned O'Sullivan of Glaun,
Schull. They lived at Lissane Lower, Drimoleague. A service medal
was awarded to him posthumously and is in the possession of his
cousins, the Looney family of Coolbawn and Church Cross,
Skibbereen. A monument, a statue of Our Lady, was blessed by Rev Fr

McSweeney, PP, Goleen. Commandant Tom Barry, author of the book *Guerilla Days in Ireland*, gave the oration. He received a tremendous ovation from the large crowd present. Commandant Sean O'Driscoll, Skibbereen, presided. A window in Lowertown Church is dedicated to his memory. McLean Terrace in Schull is named after him. A cross was erected on the south side of the main road at Cashelbeg, Gaggin, near the place where he died.

Michael John McLean was one of the many young men who gave their lives for Irish freedom. May they rest in peace.

[Note—This article was written by the late John C O'Sullivan and published by *Mizen Journal*, 1995.]

Crookhaven Lighthouse

LOWERTOWN CREAMERY

by Denis O'Neill

Lowertown Creamery, which is built in the townland of Ardravinna, was opened in 1935. The site for the building was donated free of charge by the late Robert Dukelow of Ardravinna. Mrs Mary Hunt – grandmother of Peter Hunt – and others played a major role in getting a branch of Drinagh Co-op established in the area. She travelled from house to house promoting it and encouraging local people to avail of the opportunity.

The building of the creamery was done by local labour without pay, supervised by a foreman from Drinagh Co-op. During the construction work, Tom Fitzpatrick of Ardravinna worked pumps to keep the foundations dry, as there was a lot of water at the site.

Denis O'Mahony of Caheravirane was the first supplier of milk on the first morning the branch opened, so he became number one supplier on the books. Number two supplier was John Christopher O'Sullivan and number three supplier was Barnett's. Dan Cotter of Ardravinna brought milk in buckets to the creamery, a far cry from present-day bulk tanks.

Dan Wallace was the first milk manager, Eugene Daly was the first store manager, and the first engine driver was Dan Hurley. After a few years, Dan Wallace left so Dan Hurley became milk manager, and Bill Daly got the job of engine driver.

After some time, Eugene Daly left and Jack Keohane became store manager. He was followed by John Connolly, who, when he retired, was replaced by Seamus Collins, who was promoted from assistant store manager. Seamus retired in 1994 after a lifetime of service spent in the creamery. Store managers who came after Seamus are Martin O'Martin, Billy O'Regan and the present store manager, Dan McSweeney.

The milk managers that came after Dan Hurley were Murt O'Sullivan and Michael Cadogan, respectively. As separating ceased in 1988, Michael Cadogan was the last manager in that department.

A group of Lowertown farmers who visited Drinagh Co-op in the mid-1950s.

After Bill Daly, Tom Dukelow became the next and last engine driver, as that job became redundant when separating finished. The list of names of assistant store managers included Vincent O'Regan, John C O'Sullivan, Michael Gallagher, Bernard O'Mahony, Seamus Collins, Michael Cadogan and Denis O'Callaghan, who is there to the present day. Other short-term assistants who worked in Lowertown are Timothy O'Regan, Bernard Cadogan and Jimmie Love.

The Lowertown representatives on the board of management of Drinagh Co-op were Denis Gallagher, John C O'Sullivan, who served for over 40 years, and the present holder of that position, Charles McCarthy.

Goleen 1920s

GOLEEN COMMUNITY SPORTS CENTRE

Connie O'Driscoll, chairperson of field sub-comittee

When Goleen and District Community Council was being set up in 1999 and the first elections were being organised, it was decided by the steering committee to include a 'needs survey' with the voting papers in order to get an indication from the general public of what they would like the newly elected body to achieve. The contents of those and subsequent such surveys clearly indicated a desire by the vast majority of people for facilities for the young people of our area, among other things, and in particular sports facilities.

This did not come as any great surprise because for many years a number of organisations but in particular Goleen GAA Club, who had seen the need for an alternative playing field to the area of ground on the sand dunes in the townland of Duach near Barleycove, which was used as a pitch during their long history. A number of sites had been investigated from time to time over the years, but the availability of lands along with the necessary funding required for purchase and development always consigned this to an aspiration rather than a reality. This aspiration turned to a definite need in early 2002 when the existing playing area, which the club had by virtue of the goodwill of the Cork County Council, was designated an SAC (Special Area of Conservation) by Duchas. This meant that the very necessary remedial work that was needed to be carried out on the surface was not now permissible and led to the club for all intents and purposes being evicted from this playing pitch. There was no alternative for Goleen GAA but to seek out a temporary home in a farmer's field at Gurtyowen at the other end of the parish. Likewise the local soccer club, Mizen AFC, were also moving from field to field with no permanent home ground for their ever-growing band of players and supporters.

These events in no small way helped to focus the minds of a number of the Community Council members who drew up a shortlist of possible sites in the area. Perhaps what had handicapped us over the years in seeking out such a site was the expectation that we would acquire the total area of land required from one landowner. This was proving difficult with the nature of the terrain locally and availability of such a plot in one ownership. With a slightly different outlook, the Community Council set about the task once again and very soon identified two adjoining fields in the townland of Ballysallagh adjacent to the village. One of those fields was belonging to Alex Hamilton and the other was the property of Denis O'Donoghue. When we had got an indication that both landowners would indeed agree to sell, it was decision time for the Community Council.

A meeting was convened at Heron's Cove to make the historic decision to proceed with the purchase and to identify sources of funding wherever possible. A sub-committee consisting of Connie O'Driscoll, Eamonn Sheehan, Anthony O'Callaghan, Dr Brian O'Connell, Paul O'Sullivan, Joe Hurley and Maurice Coughlan was formed to take responsibility for progressing the project onwards. This meeting was very positive and started to sort out some detail with regard to boundaries in light of the amount of land required for a full-size playing field, changing rooms and adjoining sports hall along with parking area. Full planning permission obviously was a prerequisite before final contracts could be completed and funding for purchase and development was definitely going to be the biggest challenge of all. Ballpark figures tossed around on that night indicated an overall cost somewhere between €600,000 and €850,000 for the entire project. This at first sight seemed impossible for a small parish at the far end of the Mizen peninsula but when broken down into phases over a number of years and with the possibility of funding being available from both Local Authority and central Government, along with funds raised locally and loan facilities from financial institutions, there was unanimous agreement to proceed. At the same time we were fully aware that it would be a long and difficult challenge for what was a voluntary organisation with limited experience in dealing with a project of this size.

A number of site visits were arranged to decide on the best layout of the field and building. A brief description of the original geography of the site would be that it consisted of two adjoining fields, the bigger one on the western side having a great incline with a difference in height diagonally of 30 feet from the highest point on the rock shoulder on the south-west corner to the slow-flowing stream on the northern boundary. The second field on the eastern end of the property was level but low lying and of a peaty nature. Taking all this into account and being lucky to having a few farmers and builders on our committee, decisions were quickly made that the pitch would run from east to west with the main building on the southern side of this. Rock breaking and earth moving was going to be a major challenge in order to achieve an area level enough for the playing field.

On carrying out investigation on the location we soon realised that a split-level building would lend itself ideally to the site available with dressing rooms on the lower level near the field and the sports hall and ancillary rooms overhead on the higher level. The one remaining issue was the stream on the northern side which was restricting the width of the playing area required. After protracted discussion and many site visits we eventually decided to cut the high rock face to the north of the stream and move it out 7 or 8 metres. The alternative would have been to build the pitch over the stream. Thankfully this stream did not define a boundary between two townlands because we did not want to be the ones to change the size of any townland in the parish of Goleen.

In parallel with this, on the administrative side of things, we applied for full planning permission for the entire project, along with applying for funding under the Sports Grant from the Department of Sports and Tourism. Representations were made to Cork County Council with regard to making a contribution towards the purchase price of the property and we subsequently met with the County Manager, Mr Maurice Moloney at the Mizen Vision Centre on the occasion of its official opening in March 2002. We put a strong case for funding. The County Manager in turn was quite positive and understanding, which we are sure influenced the decision of the Local Authority to grant us a substantial amount of money over a three-year time frame, which assisted us in paying off the loan facilities for the purchase of the site.

At this juncture we had a clear vision of the time scale of the entire project, which was four to five years. Phase one was to consist of pitch development and dressing room facilities with a two-year time scale. Phase two would involve the completion of the facilities on the higher level, including meeting room, kitchen, changing room, toilets, games rooms and most importantly the main sports hall, which to us would be the jewel in the crown of this complex.

Back to sums and back to figures which were added and subtracted, multiplied and divided many times to find the euros to get the project up and under way on schedule. As we mentioned earlier, one of our main sources of funding would be a National Lottery Grant which we were assured would have a good chance of being granted if we submitted a well-constructed detailed application fulfilling the three main requirements which were (1) ownership of the property (2) full planning permission granted and (3) local funding in place. One and two had been sorted and the third one we had researched and planned quietly over many meetings, which would consist of a military-style blitz throughout West Cork and further afield selling tickets to everyone possible as part of a major fundraising draw with substantial cash prizes for the winners. To carry this out successfully we realised it could not be done by just the members of the Community Council but would require a voluntary input of time and effort from many many people in our locality.

In an effort to sell the idea and to show the people that we were confident and capable of managing this major project, we decided to showcase it at an official launch at Barleycove Beach Hotel in December 2002. This was a spectacular event combining a modern-day project launch with a traditional-style Goleen social. The event attracted many politicians including Brian Crowley MEP, Denis O'Donovan TD, PJ Sheehan, MCC, John O'Shea, MCC, with special guest Tomas Mulcahy, captain of the Cork All-Ireland winning hurling team of 1990. We also had journalists present including Tom Lyons of *The Southern Star*.

The highlight of that night was the unveiling of a model of the entire complex made locally by Angelique Mueller which made our job of explaining what the end product would look like a lot easier. There were some fine speeches on the night which gave us great encouragement and then a great ould-style hooley of music, song, dance and good grub. We also launched our big draw on that evening explaining what would be involved in ticket selling all over the county in order to raise the shortfall in our funding, which we estimated at €80,000 so as to complete phase one. We were again very encouraged by the support and help offered by many local people on the night.

We got Christmas 2002 out of the way before we got down to the task of making arrangements for the selling of tickets. We were aware that it would require a big input of voluntary time from a large number of people to travel through the towns and countryside doing the difficult job of taking money from people in return for tickets with the chance of winning valuble prizes. On a cold Saturday morning in February 2003, 14 people met in Lowertown and when paired off in twos headed off to Kilbrittain area to begin our first day of ticket selling, a job that was alien to most of us but which we were willing to give a go. We already had put a local lotto in place which was drawn every Saturday night and it was there we all met up again on that particular Saturday to compare notes of success or otherwise after our day to the east. We were fairly happy but at the same time realised what a big mountain we had to climb to get anywhere near the target we set ourselves. On the next Saturday we repeated the same exercise in a different area and always met on the following Monday night to count the money, review the work and draw up plans for the following weekend. Each week, maps were marked, names were matched together, tickets supplied and instructions given to those travelling.

After a couple of weeks of modest progress it started to gain momentum with people who wanted to help ringing us instead of us ringing them and it grew and grew over the next three months to the extent that we had people out on Saturdays as usual but also on Sundays as well and any other day of the week that suited different people for different reasons. We had set a day in May to wind up the draw and by then there was hardly a man or woman in the parish who hadn't given of their time to help us. We were overwhelmed to think that a voluntary organisation could mobilise such a large number of people over so many weeks resulting in us far exceeding our target for monies raised. This revealed a community spirit in our area that many might not have realised was present and for us in the Community Council, a guaranteed reassurance that what we were doing had widespread support. The big draw culminated in a big night in the parish hall where we announced the total amount collected from ticket sales, which was in excess of €160,000. All tickets were placed in a specially constructed drum and when the winning ones were drawn they revealed names from throughout the county, evidence if it was needed, that this truly was a vast exercise and hugely successful. A couple of Sundays later we brought the winners to Goleen to present them with their prizes and then we sat and relaxed and regaled with stories about our experiences as we travelled the countryside over the previous weeks and months.

In relation to the applications we had submitted to the Department of Sports for lottery funding, a decision on such applications were delayed that year. However, we lost no opportunity to talk up our plans to anyone we met that we thought might influence our case, including the Minister for Sport, John O'Donoghue, who came to Goleen in June of 2003, and we left Minister O'Donoghue in no doubt that any monies he would sanction for us would be spent well and wisely for the youth of our area. Then we waited for a decision and were relieved and delighted at the announcement that we had been allocated the largest grant in the county with a figure of €150,000 from the Department of Sport and a further €30,000 from the Clar

Programme. This money would only be paid out when stages of work were completed and invoices submitted.

We had the purchase and legal transfer of the property completed by that stage and then on 27th August, a historic day for us, the diggers moved in and the real work began. The first job was the removal and stacking of topsoil and then the intricate job of laying the network of underground drains to sort out the section of the grounds that were of a peaty nature. We then started to excavate rockfill along the north and south boundaries of the site, the latter section also forming the foundation for the dressing rooms and sports hall complex. The next step was a cut-and-fill process in the playing field area to try and achieve a pretty level surface. This having been completed in December 2003, we took a break and allowed the whole area to settle for a couple of months. This gave us time to take stock and concentrate on preparing the layout of the building site. We had initially considered awarding the full contract for the building to a construction company and we invited tenders for same. However, when we did get back the prices it was obvious to us that we could not afford to go that route. We then decided to break it up into smaller contracts for the different sections of the project and that we would act as project managers ourselves and also purchase most of the materials required. We were well aware that this would require an enormous amount of voluntary time but when budgets were compared it would save us anywhere from €100,000 to €150,000 when all would be completed.

In order to help us to make some major decisions with regard to internal layout of dressing rooms and sports hall and other aspects such as lighting, heating, ventilation, wall and floor finishes, a group of us set off one Sunday early in 2004 to look at complexes from Skibbereen to Youghal. We met some very helpful people everywhere we visited, each of them in their own way having gone through the same process that we were then experiencing. Throughout May and June of 2004 the major amount of the ground works in the playing area were sorted with all cross drains having been completed and subsoil laid over the whole section. Then came the very meticulous job of respreading the topsoil over that and getting it ready for the sowing of grass seed. This job was completed on 31st July and as if we ordered it or the Lord just knew we needed it, the rain came that night and some of next day as well and so within three weeks we had a lovely blanket of grass. Fencing was completed over the next month to secure the property. We conceded a strip on the eastern boundary for necessary widening and improvement to the Corelacka road.

The first loads of concrete were poured on site in October of that year for the construction of retaining walls and foundations, these being the first steps in the erecting of the main building. The portal frame for this was eventually erected in March 2005, having been sitting on site for two months. Once erected we were ready to commence block work on the lower level so that the dressing rooms, referee's room and store would be completed and ready for use at the same time as the playing field would be used for competitive games. 23rd April 2005 was another red letter day for us in the Community Council, as this was the first time the new field was used by our local teams for training. The first competitive games took place there that August to accommodate the festival soccer and GAA competitions. The playing surface met with universal approval which was a great source of satisfaction for us.

By now the block work on the whole building had been more or less completed with sub-floors laid and doors and windows fitted. We had an enclosed building by Christmas 2005 with the first stage works of plumbing and wiring in place. We had also erected basic flood lighting on the southern side of the field, adequate for training purposes on those winter and spring evenings.

One of the other really proud days for us involved in the project was Sunday, 13th November 2005, when a West Cork under-12 final was played between the home team, Mizen Rovers, and D Ó Mathúnas with our boys and girls winning a very exciting match. What a wonderful way to christen our new field. Early 2006 and a reality check for us again in that we were finding out, similar to most people who have ever done a building job, that the biggest costs are in the finishing stages, with the result that our funds were running low.

We were now well into phase two of our project and there was no turning back. Even with the continuing generosity of our local people and others through the weekly lotto, funds to complete a state-of-the-art sports hall along with training pitch, floodlighting, final landscaping and driveways would require a new application for National Lottery monies from the 2006 programme and anywhere else monies could be sourced, including West Cork Leader and Cork County Council. We applied to them all and were successful at varying levels with each. This enabled us to complete the entrance and external groundworks along with ball retaining, tarmacadam and other remaining fencing work. We also purchased numerous items of equipment necessary in the use of the sporting and leisure facilities at the centre.

The sports floor of the main hall was a major challenge of our committee and having deliberated and consulted widely we opted for a seamless polyurethane product supplied from mainland Europe and fitted by four highly trained men from the city of Warsaw in Poland. A beautiful new fitted kitchen along with all necessary appliances for social events were purchased along with furniture and other seating. We also erected an external seated viewing area to the west of the main building. This we decided to call 'The Michael Burchill Stand' dedicated to the memory of this fine young man and athlete who captained the U21 Goleen football team, winners of the South West Cork Championship of 1999. His sudden and untimely death in January 2003 left a great void in the sporting annals of our area. The late Michael was from the townland of Lackanakea near Crookhaven.

The entire project was completed in July 2007 just inside the five-year time scale we projected at the outset in 2002. We have in it a quality and modern state-of-the-art sports complex, both indoor and outdoor, which was proved during the early part of 2007 when most pitches were closed, and Goleen was chosen as the venue for many important GAA championship games with teams and officials fulsome in their praise of the facilities made available to them. This keeping in mind that it was used most Sundays throughout the winter by the local soccer team Mizen AFC and others. This makes us, the field sub-committee of the Community Council – which includes five of the original committee along with Denis Downey, Tommy Jermyn, Tim Barnett, Denis O'Neill and Vicky Greenway and all of those others who have been involved over the five years – really proud that as a voluntary group we have been capable of successfully organising and managing such a major project. We are delighted and very proud that we have a facility that the people of this area can be justly proud of and that hopefully will be used for many generations to come. We also hope that this landmark development will act as a springboard for more and greater developments and achievements for the area in years to come and in particular for our young people, who as ever are the future of our parish and our greatest asset.

OUR PAST POSTMEN

Over 50 years a-posting
by Jim Cluskey

His name is Michael Supple. And the 'supple' applies in another way, too, because, during the past 54 years, he has covered a total distance of between 470,000 and 480,000 miles, give or take the odd thousand or so.

Michael, of Gortnacarriga on the Mizen peninsula, was a postman from the age of 16 and his round covered an area of some 25 miles. Now, a young-looking, jolly man of 70, he has retired and a part of life for an older generation will never be the same again.

When Michael first started delivering the post, he worked a three-day week and his pay, he recalls, was 8/9d a week, roughly 60 cents in today's money. When he went on a four-day week, as the service expanded, his pay rose to 12/- a week, which would be 90 cents at present. But he had always a bit of farming to supplement his income, which, even with the value of money in those days, was clearly just as well.

For the first ten or twelve years, he did his rounds on foot. But things got better when he changed 'shanks-mare' for a horse, even though it may not have been exactly the pony express. And from the horse he graduated to a bicycle – a mode of transport he retained until his retirement. But he recalls, too, getting down on his hands and knees to deliver the mail – that was when, in storm conditions, he crawled from the mainland across the narrow bridge, high over rocks and pounding seas, to the Mizen Lighthouse. The analogy to the motto of the famous Pony Express was there: 'The mail must get through.'

In the 54 years that he serviced the area, Michael became like a member of the family in many a remote homestead. And, especially in the early days, he was also one of the main links with the outside world, spreading the everyday news of life in the peninsula.

A career like that does not end unnoticed, and Michael and his wife Bridget were guests of honour at a party in the Barleycove Hotel,

Michael Supple handing a letter to Denis Downey on the last day of his rounds. In the background, part of Lissagriffin Lake, known sometimes as the Swan Lake, and on the pole is the furthest south postbox in Ireland.
(M Minihane)

when people from all over his area turned up to present Michael with a colour television. The presentation was made on their behalf by Mr Joe O'Sullivan, Postmaster, Skibbereen, who put into words the feeling of the people for a lifetime of dedicated service.

Just a Memory
– Michael Sheehan, Goleen's finest postman
by Jonathan Smyth

The village of Goleen is situated in West Cork. The mixture of coastline, stonewalls and mountainous scenery make Goleen one of the most beautiful places to visit. Farming is the community's main profession and, in the past, cattle fairs were often held. The village contains a harbour known as Heron's Cove. In Irish Goleen is 'an Goilín', which means 'a little inlet'. Like many rural places, the post office has remained an important feature of communication in the area.

Mr Michael Sheehan was one of the longest-serving postmen at Goleen. He was born in June 1910. He had three brothers who later emigrated to America. In 1933, Michael began working as a postman for

Michael Sheehan, Goleen postman for nearly 50 years.

Goleen Post Office. He delivered the local post for nearly 50 years. In 1937, he married his wife Katherine and they had a family of four children.

Times were tough with the introduction of 'rationing' during World War II. Rationing affected business in Ireland. The shortage of bicycle tyres caused problems for the postman. Michael ended up delivering the post by horseback and sometimes on foot. Rationing continued to the early 1950s.

At half past seven each morning, Michael would start by milking and feeding his cows. Afterwards, dressed neatly in postman's uniform, he then cycled the 2.5 miles to Goleen PO. The post office was located in a grocery shop named Harrington's. The telephone operator also worked from a section in the same shop. Michael began at about nine o'clock in the morning. In about six minutes he would deliver the village post before cycling to the surrounding townlands. Often, he would stop at the local creamery where he could hand farmers their mail, thereby saving time on the overall trip.

The route had many steep hills and he would have to walk some of the journey. He cycled 27 miles per day, for six days per week. Michael worked solidly for seven hours without a break until his rounds were completed. He finished work in the afternoon around four o'clock.

For many years, he was instantly recognisable with his black push-bike, the postbag strapped over his shoulder, and the letter bag slung on the handlebars. He would oil the bicycle twice a week in preparation for his daily travel. He went out in all weathers and was only sick once in all his years of service. In the wettest weather, Michael wore the yellow oil-skins to keep the rain from soaking his clothes.

Goleen is close to Mizen Head and during gale force winds, he had to keep a steady hand when steering the bike. After a day's work, he attended to farming matters at home before he finished up for the evening.

The postman was a welcome visitor to country folk, who chatted about many subjects including the weather. Many of the postmen did 'good deeds' by obliging to do small messages for people in remote areas. Michael Sheehan is remembered as a cheerful man who enjoyed his job. He greeted friends and neighbours with a gentlemanly raise of his finger to tip his hat.

In 1975, Michael was interviews for Irish television. Excerpts from the interview have been featured in various documentaries over the years. In August 2005, TG4 featured him in one of its programmes. At the time, his friends estimated that over the years he had used 22 bicyclces, 240 brake pads and 96 tyres.

They also calculated that 'he cycled an equivalent distance of ten times around the equator and that was doing the same unchanging route day after day'. By the 1970s, his colleague were using post vans and motorbikes.

Michael had good health all his life and continued his job until 1980. Mr Michael Sheehan, the postman from Goleen, retired aged 70. For many, his visits will remain a lifelong memory.

At Giants Causeway. During the 1990s a coach load of Goleen parishioners used to go on a weeks tour of the country, having been in each of the 32 counties and a week in Wales. During that period their title was 'Discover Ireland Group'.

THE PARISH IN THE YEAR AD 2010

by Pat McCarthy

Gurthdove, Goleen, April 1996

These thoughts are only my personal opinions as to the way we are heading towards the year AD 2010 at the present time. It is a fine thing to stop and take stock of where we're going and if it's wrong to try and head in a different direction. Like clearing a house for the stations – keep what is good and useful and throw out what's not wanted. This competition gives us a fine way to express ourselves and I hope that many of us take the opportunity to speak up. Here then are some of my thoughts.

A lot of surnames in the parish will have died out by 2010. My honest opinion is that the faith and morals of the people who are still here will be very weak. Many are now not practising their religion, be they Church of Ireland or Catholic, and it will get worse. A death rate of around 30 people per year in a parish of some 700 people is a sad situation. Of the native people that are living in 2010 in the parish, half of them will be dependent on government and EU subsidies and pensions.

It will be a population of the elderly, the way things are going. The people who have families now, their sons and daughters will not be able to continue in their parents' way of life, due to the rules and the regulations of the EU. The excessively high standard of hygiene required by this authority will destroy the small farmer and the small businessman alike. It will also destroy the health of the parish in the end, for the people will have no immunity to disease due to the sealing and packaging and sanitising of all food. This lack of natural immunity will mean that we will rely more on pills and medicines from the doctor, if there is one in the parish by that time, which I very much doubt. Wildlife will be destroyed too; as the land is reclaimed, the bogs will be drained and the frogs and insects and plants will go. The ancient ways that our forefathers trod will disappear forever. The briars and the blackberries, the copogues, the rare flowers and herbs of the Mizen that were used to prevent illnesses and flus, will be swept away due, too, to the poisonous liquids used in farming to meet the common market regulations. The folklore, stories and customs of the parish which are almost gone, will be gone altogether.

The district will be taken over by tourists, and foreigners will be living in our home places, where they will neither relax nor relate nor communicate. Marriage will be rarer and there will be more divorce and broken marriages, more illegitimate children and most likely no priest in the parish to marry, bury or baptise them. Crime will increase due to the mixed race of people tyring to find some way to live together with neither language or customs in common. It was in the prophesy that the Irish would become strangers in their land. As it is, it's grand to see the tourists come in the summertime and we enjoy the foreigners and retired folk living around. But at some time in the future, a balance should be struck as to numbers in relation to the native people. There will possibly be only one national school in the parish by 2010. The business premises of Goleen village will be owned by more companies, rather than families. Most of the produce coming into our district is coming from other parts of the Ireland and from abroad too. It would be a good thing if our highly educated young people could tap into production here in Goleen, rather than using their skills in foreign lands.

> Our people will be known
> More by their number than name
> By EU regulations
> What a terrible shame.

> With TV and videos
> And computers galore
> We're not fully using
> Our brains anymore.

Another thing that has changed and will continue doing so, unless common sense will become part of us again, are the daily conversation and neighbourly ways of the people. In the morning the birds still sing in the trees but the people have fallen silent for some reason. As a boy, I remember neighbouring women hanging their washing and singing to their hearts' content. Men would go to their fields jigging and humming away like bees in a bottle. Now it's the roar of machines and blasts of exhausts that would blind your eyes and deafen your ears, with the haste and hurry to gather more to their store. And I wonder if many take the time to thank God for the fine morning and their health as each day is a new day and a gift from the almighty God.

Michael Donovan of Dunkelly, who died 30 years ago, used to say there is amusement in sport and joy in labour found. It is easy to forget what the old people never forgot, when they asked God to help and protect them for the day as they stood in the field before starting the work each day. Will there be any with this common sense left by the year 2010? People say they have no time today, but there are the same 24 hours in the day that there have always been.We can use them or abuse them. Family life in the neighbourhood and in the home is changing altogether. Twenty years ago they were talking about the living and praying for the day. Any house that you went into you were welcome as the flowers of May, as one of their own. This welcome is not in the homes any more. People prefer TV and discussing their own affairs rather than other people's conversation and stories. The style and the wit, the kind nature and hospitality that marked our parish will be lost to a very great extent in the future; replaced by fax machines and the internet.

It is very important that the present-day mothers and fathers should be handing down to the children our knowledge, histories and traditional morals, for they will be in charge of the parish by the year 2010. Let us hope they will keep their faith and lands and that they continue to show our way of life to the people who come from far and wide. Remember that these foreigners come because they have lost these things in their own home places and can still find them here in this parish. Our lands and coastlines and the ancient paths that we ever trod are being sold, wired and fenced and by 2010 we could easily find ourselves taken over by foreigners again, and this time through our own greed and with the way back blocked. It would be in proper order if no planning permissions were given without paths round coastlines, and paths and rights of way to our ancient places, like the Three Castles, in order that the people can continue to walk this lovely land freely as we have always done. The EU and tourists put easy money into our pockets and it's mighty easy to sell our birthrights for a mess of potage.

We survived the Famine
With suffering and pain
We fought for our freedom
With honour and fame

The EU is looming
And with its soft paw
We are taking its promises
Its grants and much more

To wind up – and these are only my points of view, as I am one in a thousand, but – I hope that my thoughts fit in with others' in the parish. We pray that the people that are here in AD 2010 will have as much time for God as for earthly things.

St Patrick's Roman Catholic Church, Goleen sometime before 1950 with old spire.

MARCONI'S WIRELESS TELEGRAPH STATION AT CROOKHAVEN

by Michael Sexton and Claire Barrett

Introduction

The last two decades of the nineteenth century ushered in a spectacular series of scientific advances in physical science, notably in electricity and magnetism. By that time the inter-relationship between these two intriguing topics of natural philosophy had been established theoretically in 1864 by the Scotsman James Clark Maxwell and the related phenomena were then classified as being on an 'electromagnetic' (EM) nature.

In 1888 the German scientist Heinrich Hertz clearly demonstrated that electromagnetic waves (now called radio waves), produced by a series of sparks, were identical with light waves, except for wavelength, and could be transmitted and received across a laboratory.

Guglielmo Marconi (1874–1937)

The stage was now set for the obvious application, i.e., transmission 'without wires' but it was not until 1895 that the feasibility of meaningful transmissions was clearly demonstrated well beyond the confines of a house by the young Irish-Italian Guglielmo Macroni.

Marconi was the son of a prosperous Italian businessman and his second wife, Anna. Anna was a a member of the well-known Jameson family – of distillery fame – and was born at Daphne Castle, Enniscorthy, Co Wexford. She studied music a Bologna Conservatory and there married a widower, Guiseppe Marconi. The second son of this marriage was Guglielmo, born in April 1874. His early education was by private tuition and he also studied physics and chemistry at Bologna under Professor Augusto Righi, who was himself one of the pioneers of experiments in electromagnetism.

Marconi came across an account of Hertz's experiments in the summer of 1894. He commenced experiments in the winter of 1894 on his father's estate near Pontecchio with a feeling of near disbelief that no one had grasped the commerical possibility of Hertzian waves. 'When I started my first experiments with Hertzian waves,' he is quoted as saying, 'I could scarcely believe it was possible that their application to useful purposes could have escaped the notice of eminent scientists.'

He quickly succeeded in transmitting dots and dashes through rooms of the house using conventional equipment, and had moved outdoors by the summer of 1895. In an effort to increase the capacitance of his transmitter, he hit upon the significance of using an elevated metal plate situated at the top of a pole and connected through a spark-gap at the transmitter to a similar plate in the ground. This 'grounded antenna' not only increased the capacitance but also extended the distance over which the radiation could be detected. He also replaced the spark-gap in the receiver, which limited the range to the order of yards, by a device known as a 'coherer'. This consisted of a cylinder of metal filings, the resistance of which diminished substantially under the influence of radio waves and was inserted in an external circuit containing a printing recorder.

Having succeeded in receiving signals over a distance of 1.5 miles, Marconi, then only 22, travelled to Britain with his mother, arriving in February 1896. His mother, whose family was well known in influential circles, had determined to secure financial and technical aid for his venture. Through her efforts, Marconi demonstrated his apparatus with remarkable success in the presence of Sir William Preece, engineer-in-chief of the British Post Office (the same who had earlier ridiculed Hughe's demonstration in 1879), who very quickly decided to place his very considerable support at the young inventor's disposal. On 2nd June 1896, Marconi disclosed the details of his system by filing a specification for the first patent ever granted in wireless telegraphy.

From that time onwards, Marconi carried out a considerable number of transmit-receive tests over land, over sea, ship-to-shore and ship-to-ship, in Britain and Ireland, all the time improving his primitive spark-gap transmissions using tapping keys. The most exciting success was, of course, the transmissions from Poldhu in Cornwall to a number of stations in Newfoundland and Nova Scotia in December 1901.

Within a year, the Marconi Wireless Telegraph Company was formed with the aid of £100,000 raised from hard-headed British businessmen. However, the company did not prosper for a considerable time – to be exact, until 1912 when the attention of the world was focused on the vital role enacted by the wireless operators of the ill-fated *Titanic* in transmitting distress signals before she sank following the collision with a iceberg.

Marconi in Ireland

From the outset Marconi realised the significance of the geographical location in Ireland in relation to North America and (perhaps, encouraged by his Irish mother) carried out much of his early fieldwork in Ireland.

Before considering the Crookhaven station in detail, I would like to make some comments on Marconi's other activities in Ireland at that time.

Rathlin – Ballycastle (May 1898)

Following successful demonstrations in Britain in 1896, Lloyds of London, in May 1896, commissioned Marconi to set up a line between Rathlin Island and Ballycastle, Co Antrim, to advise ships regarding unpredictable weather conditions in the exposed waters beyond the island. This was the world's first commercial use of wireless.

Kingstown Regatta (July 1889)

Perhaps the best way of describing this is to reproduce Marconi's own words during a lecture to the Institution of Electrical Engineers, London, in 1899, and subsequently published in the institution's journal. It was, in fact, Marconi's first paper in English.[1]

'Following this, in July we were requested by a Dublin paper, the *Daily Express*, to report from the high seas the results and incidents of the Kingstown Regatta. In order to do this, we erected a land station, by the kind permission of the harbour master at Kingstown, in his grounds, where a pole 110 ft high was placed. A steamer, the Flying Huntress, was chartered to follow the racing yachts, the instruments being placed in the cabin. The height of the vertical wire attainable by the mast was 75 ft. A telephone was fixed from our land station at Kingstown to the Express office in Dublin, and as the messages came from the ship they were telephoned to Dublin, and published in succeeding editions of the evening papers.

'The relative positions of the various yachts were thus surely signally while the races were in progress, sometimes over a distance of 10 miles, and were published long before the yachts had returned to harbour. During the several days the system was in use between the tug and the land station, over 700 messages were sent and received, none requiring to be repeated. On trying longer distances it was found that with a height of 80 ft on the ship and the same height as already stated on land, it was possible to communicate up to a distance of 25 miles, and it is worthy of note in the case that the curvature of the earth intervened very considerably at such distances between the positions. On one occasion, on a regatta day, I had the pleasure of the company of Professor GF Fitzpatrick, of Trinity College, Dublin, on the ship, who, as would be expected, took a very great interest in proceedings.'

Clifden Wireless Station (1907–1922)

Until the development in 1922–1924 of the short wave directional propogation (i.e., radio beams) and their unique properties for long-distance communication, the results of experiments at Poldhu and elsewhere directed all development effort towards higher power and longer wavelengths to increase the working range. This entailed increasingly larger aerial systems and the necessity for more ground space that was available at Poldhu. Clifden, Co Galway, was chosen as providing ample ground area, as well as the shortest feasible wireless link with Glace Bay station on Cape Breton Island off Nova Scotia in Canada.

By the standards of the time, Clifden station was a massive affair with eight masts over 200 ft high, a generating plant providing an output of 300kW at 20,000 volts (turf-fired from the local bog on which a special narrow gauge railway was laid) and employing at its peak a permanent staff of over 150. In fact, the station was the first point-to-point fixed wireless station in the world.

The Clifden station undoubtedly lifted Marconi's fortunes out of potential bankruptcy with profits arising from it transatlantic commercial communications until its abrupt demise during the 1922–1923 Civil War when it was summarily destroyed by irregular Republican forces on the pretext of it being a British concern, the rights of which, they claimed, were withheld under the terms of the Anglo–Irish Treaty of 1921.

Marconi's Wireless Station at Crookhaven (1901–1914)

Following Marconi's preliminary field trials referred to previously, together with successful wireless linking with a ship 18 miles off the coast in December 1897, Marconi ordered the construction of several small wireless stations around the southern English and Irish coasts. One of these was at Crookhaven, Co Cork, situated on Brow Head, located between the village of Crookhaven and Barleycove.

It has been quite difficult to obtain much authoritative information on what exactly was accomplished by the early Marconi personnel at Crookhaven. This is compounded by the fact that there had been a Reuters news telegraph station there earlier and even a Napoleonic signal tower dating from around 1807, the ruin of which is still standing. Furthermore, Lloyds and the GPO also had installations there at one stage. As noted by Walter McGrath in the *Cork Examiner*, 1974, in the course of two memorable articles celebrating the centenary of Marconi's birth, a study of all the news gathering and transmissions to and from Brow Head over many generations would be fruitful indeed.[2]

However, the Crookhaven station got off to a flying start in June 1901 when, soon after its opening and in the presence of Marconi himself, morse signals were clearly received from Poldhu in Cornwall, 225 miles distant. This not only confirmed the station's range as being the planned 300 miles using a spark-gap transmitter and coherer detectors, but the received signals were of such strength that Marconi felt quite confident of 'bridging the Atlantic' – which he duly did only six months later.

It is clear that Marconi visited Crookhaven on at least three occasions, using the Skibbereen to Schull light railway for part of the journey and calling to the offices of the *Cork Examiner*.

Notwithstanding the scarcity of information relating to Crookhaven, the author was forwarded an article by the Marconi Co., Chelmsford, written in 1911 by one of the operators (WH Leach).[3] The following extracts give a very good contemporary insight into the workings of the station at that time.

'There were at that date few sea-going vessels fitted with wireless apparatus, and the comparatively easy life of the operator on duty there in those days may be gauged from the fact that fifty messages from in-going and out-going steamers was considered a great feat. The actual telegraphic work was hardly sufficient to keep the operators busy at all times, but in following the developments in wireless telegraphy these operators were kept constantly interested. A change has, however, come over the place. The magnetic detector has been introduced, and Crookhaven has sprung into prominence as a wireless station. By reason of its geographical situation, all ships coming from the west and bound for a European port enter into communication with Crookhaven, and that station is busily employed, night and day, in sending and receiving messages.

'As Crookhaven is the first station with which the homeward-bound American liners communicate it is naturally a busy station. By the aid of wireless all arrangements are made for the arrival of the ships, the landing and entraining of the passengers and mails, whilst hundreds of private messages to and from passengers are dealt with. Messages are also received from the Fastnet Lighthouse, which is fitted with wireless, reporting the passing of sailing ships and steamers. These messages are sent by vessels not fitted with wireless by means of signals to the Fastnet, thence by wireless to Crookhaven, whence they are forwarded to Lloyd's and to the owners of the vessels.'

No paper on Marconi's Crookhaven station would be complete without reference to Arthur (Daddy) Nottage, the Englishman who became both a legend and an institution in his own lifetime in Crookhaven – indeed in West Cork – where he live amongst friends for some 70 years, being the owner of the Welcome Inn public house.

He had an extraordinary career and indeed as a youth of only 20 he was a major link between Europe and North America via incoming ships passing Crookhaven. He found himself in the exalted position in 1904 when he arrived in Crookhaven to work, on a shift basis with one other man, as a Marconi telegrapher. Until 1914, he operated the Morse code apparatus from Brow Head, with his salary for such responsible work being a reputed generous £1 per week!

The present writer had the very good fortune to meet Mr Nottage in Crookhaven some years before his death at the age of 90 in 1974. He still had handwritten log books from the station recording the daily events and explained the workings of wireless during that far-off period to a very interested audience that day in the Welcome Inn.

By 1914 the Crookhaven station was beginning to lose its usefulness due to the limited range and it is understood that Marconi sold the wireless rights to Cable and Wireless Ltd on Valentia Island, Co Kerry. World War I gave it another lease of life.

Finally, the last station master in Schull, James O'Sullivan is on record as stating that the Irregular Republican forces (as in Clifden) burnt the premises in 1922. It is also known that Mr O'Sullivan salvaged an oil driven engine used for providing power to the transmitters at that time and it is thought that this engine still exists, probably in the Schull area. It should be stated that, unlike Clifden, the Crookhaven station had been occasionally used by the Royal Navy to contact its ships from its base in Berehaven. For example, some documents are still extant for such transmissions in 1908. This fact may have been an excuse for the destruction of the station by the Irregulars, as the Royal Navy remained in Berehaven until 1938.

Thus ended the short-lived but very intriguing existence of Crookhaven Wireless Station. It was a significant element in North Atlantic ship-to-shore communications in the early twentieth century and its location clearly shows Guglielmo Marconi's sharp commercial enterprise. It is, perhaps, fitting that in these centenary years of recalling Marconi's great achievements, Crookhaven should now be given its rightful place in the early history of wireless telegraphy.

From left, Claire Barrett, Baroness Elettra Marconi Giovanalli and Róisín Barrett.

Article from *West Cork News*, Friday 7th August 1998:

The Baroness Marconi comes back 'home' to Crookhaven

When Baroness Elettra Marconi Giovanalli, daughter of the father of wireless Guglielmo Marconi, came home to Crookhaven, a party was a certainty.

And a party there was at Marconi House, now a guest house and restaurant run for the past 21 years by Claire Barrett.

Marconi House was originally the Crookhaven post office. The post office moved to the village in 1901 to facilitate Marconi in his radio experiments in wireless telegraphy. From the radio station he set up in Crookhaven, Marconi succeeded for the first time in transmitting signals across the Atlantic.

Eventually, the Crookhaven station was moved to Valentia. Marconi spent 11 months in Crookhaven in 1901 and his family always heard about his happy time there.

Baroness Elettra, his only surviving child, is now in her seventies and lives in Rome. The baroness jumped at the chance of coming to Ireland for the opening of the new broadcasting museum at Cork City Gaol and could not let the occasion pass without a visit to Crookhaven.

Claire Barrett hosted a lunch for her there at Marconi House and about 20 people attended. Afterwards they went to Nottage's in the village. The late Arthur Nottage worked as an assistant to Marconi during his time at Crookhaven. The party also visited the radio mast site at Brow Head.

Róisín Barrett, daughter of Claire Barrett, did a project on Marconi and Baroness Elettra took a copy of it. Her father, she said, had a knack of always selecting beautiful sites for his experiments and Crookhaven was the most beautiful of all.

Centenary of Radio:

Guglielmo Marconi was the man who took radio communication from an experimental stage to a practical form of communication, successfully transmitting over a distance of 1 kilmotre in 1895. Prior to this, many eminent scientists had experimented with radio waves, but with very limited success. In 1896, Marconi patented his apparatus and in 1897 formed his Wireless, Telegraphy and Signal Company Ltd (now GEC Marconi Ltd) – this was made possible by relatives on his mother's side, members of the Irish Jameson Family, better known for their whiskey distillery.

Assisted by investment from Jameson Davis, Marconi continued to increase the range and power of his equipment, and he went on to prove the effectiveness of radio communication in commercial as well as military and other applications.

Marconi established many stations in Ireland, most notably that at Clifden, Co Galway, from which transatlantic transmissions were sent.

The stamps are in se-tenant format – the first, which is being jointly issued by Germany, Italy, The Vatican, San Marino and Ireland, features a portrait with his 1896 apparatus, was designed by Professor Ernst Junger. The second, showing an old radio dial with the radio stations of the participating countries featured, was designed by Stephen Young, who also designed the first day cover. The stamps and first day cover were printed by Irish Security Stamp Printing Ltd.

Acknowledgements

Sincere thanks is due to Mr Paddy Clarke of RTÉ Archives for his great interest in providing hitherto unpublished material; to Mr Ted Crosbie, chief executive, Examiner Publications, for providing newspaper articles relating to Marconi from the *Cork Examiner* files; and to Mrs Martin, Marconi House Restaurant, Crookhaven, for information relating to Royal Naval activities on Brow Head.

References

1. Marconi, G, 'Wireless Technology', *Journal of Institution of Electrical Engineers*, 28, pp. 273–318, 1899.
2. McGrath, W, 'Ireland's Part in the Marconi Dream', *Cork Examiner*, 1974.

3. Leach, HW, 'The Human Element at a Wireless Station: Life at Crookhaven', *The Marconigraph*, pp. 23–25, September 1911.

Bibliography

Two very recent volumes relating not only to Marconi but to the overall picture during the nineteenth century and with particular attention to the controversy (still raging!) concerning the claims of Marconi, Popov and Lodge for being 'first in the field' of wireless are:

1. Garrat, GR, *The Early History of Radio: from Faraday to Marconi*, Institution of Electrical Engineers, London, 1994.
2. Rowlands, P and Wilson, JP, *Oliver Lodge and the Invention of Radio*, PD Publications, Liverpool, 1994.

Farmers at Lissigriffin stop of "Travelling Creamery" 1946.Front row L-R: Jack Reilly, Tady O'Leary, Dan McCarthy, Maurice Downey, Dan Sullivan, Bill Neville, Joe Goggin, Tim Sheehan, Middle row Tadg Wilcox, John O'Driscoll, Billy Supple, Jack O' Driscoll. Back row: Albert Donovan, Tom Barry, Timmie Reilly, John Collins, Tim Cotter. The "Travelling Creamery" can be seen in the back of the picture.

POPULATIONS OF GOLEEN TOWNLANDS

by Denis Downey

Hereunder can be found the number of people and houses in each of the 92 townlands of the parish in the years 1841–1851 and 1997–2002, as supplied by the Central Statistics Office. Houses that were unoccupied on the night of the Census forms being filled were not included. The total population and houses in the parish in the four following censuses is as follows:

Year	1841	1851	1997	2002
Population	12,594	6,553	1,071	1,163
Houses	2,191	1,241	870	440

Some interesting findings can be found in the censuses; for example, in the 1851 census, there were people living in every townland in the parish. In 1997 there were 11 unoccupied townlands and in 2002 there were 15. Another interesting finding is that in the two earlier censuses, the average number per household is between five and six, in 1997 it was one to two, and in 2002 it was two to three people per household.

The townlands of Goleen Parish

	1841	1851	1997	2002	2002 as % of 1841
Altar					
Population	205	196	5	6	3%
Houses	36	38	12	5	14%
Arderrawinny					
Population	336	169	31	38	11%
Houses	7	7	4	0	0%
Arduslough					
Population	39	34	0	0	0%
Houses	7	7	4	0	0%

	1841	1851	1997	2002	2002 as % of 1841
Ballybrack					
Population	122	70	3	6	5%
Houses	21	12	2	1	5%
Ballydivlin					
Population	462	302	49	59	13%
Houses	81	59	49	23	28%
Ballynaule					
Population	27	31	2	0	0%
Houses	4	4	2	0	0%
Ballyrisode					
Population	371	141	39	43	12%
Houses	73	27	25	16	22%
Ballyvoge Beg					
Population	55	21	3	2	4%
Houses	9	3	1	2	22%
Ballyvoge More					
Population	83	53	11	17	20%
Houses	12	7	10	5	42%
Ballyvonane					
Population	82	37	0	0	0%
Houses	13	6	7	0	0%
Balteen (West)					
Population	187	114	14	14	7%
Houses	32	23	14	7	22%
Balteen (East)					
Population	59	30	3	5	8%
Houses	12	4	2	1	8%
Barnatonicane					
Population	128	34	7	12	9%
Houses	20	6	4	6	30%
Beakeen					
Population	86	30	6	6	7%
Houses	12	5	5	3	25%
Boulysallagh					
Population	100	81	20	30	30%
Houses	18	17	30	12	67%
Caher					
Population	194	74	16	10	5%
Houses	34	14	8	4	12%

	1841	1851	1997	2002	2002 as % of 1841
Caheravirane					
Population	65	37	11	17	26%
Houses	13	5	5	5	38%
Caherolickane					
Population	146	35	6	13	9%
Houses	26	15	5	4	15%
Callaros Eighter					
Population	128	85	37	34	27%
Houses	25	18	23	12	48%
Callaros Oughter					
Population	263	131	7	16	6%
Houses	49	27	8	6	12%
Cannawee					
Population	96	36	15	16	17%
Houses	16	8	10	7	44%
Carrigacat and Milleen					
Population	289	106	11	13	4%
Houses	48	24	15	4	8%
Carrigacurriheen					
Population	60	26	0	0	0%
Houses	10	4	1	0	0%
Carrigeengour					
Population	48	30	7	9	19%
Houses	8	4	2	2	25%
Carrigmanus					
Population	54	16	19	12	22%
Houses	7	2	5	4	57%
Cashelfean					
Population	379	128	26	31	8%
Houses	74	30	16	11	15%
Castlemehigan					
Population	88	42	5	3	3%
Houses	15	8	6	2	13%
Castlepoint					
Population	45	16	4	4	9%
Houses	5	3	3	3	60%
Cloghanaculleen					
Population	187	114	28	22	12%
Houses	31	22	14	10	32%

	1841	1851	1997	2002	2002 as % of 1841
Cloghanalehid					
Population	46	7	0	0	0%
Houses	6	1	1	0	0%
Cloghane					
Population	100	48	0	0	0%
Houses	13	7	3	0	0%
Clogher					
Population	13	10	8	6	46%
Houses	1	1	3	3	300%
Coomfarna					
Population	12	10	2	0	0%
Houses	2	2	1	0	0%
Coorlacka					
Population	138	87	20	16	12%
Houses	22	15	6	4	18%
Corran Beg					
Population	81	48	4	2	2%
Houses	12	9	6	1	8%
Corran More					
Population	146	53	11	8	5%
Houses	24	8	11	4	17%
Cove					
Population	254	53	13	7	3%
Houses	49	10	7	4	8%
Crookhaven					
Population	472	404	39	59	13%
Houses	97	79	72	25	26%
Derryfunshion					
Population	114	36	1	1	1%
Houses	19	6	5	1	5%
Derryleary					
Population	192	73	26	24	13%
Houses	34	14	7	6	18%
Dough					
Population	87	29	1	1	1%
Houses	14	6	5	1	7%
Drinane					
Population	94	60	13	18	19%
Houses	16	12	10	5	31%

	1841	1851	1997	2002	2002 as % of 1841
Drishane					
Population	181	120	20	15	8%
Houses	27	24	14	6	22%
Dunkelly East					
Population	199	32	10	10	5%
Houses	35	5	16	3	9%
Dunkelly Middle					
Population	126	40	4	1	1%
Houses	25	10	4	1	4%
Dunkelly West					
Population	85	75	6	9	11%
Houses	17	15	3	5	29%
Dunlough					
Population	67	52	4	1	1%
Houses	9	9	2	1	11%
Dumanus East					
Population	460	165	14	25	5%
Houses	81	33	9	9	11%
Dunmanus West					
Population	424	152	20	21	5%
Houses	83	28	15	7	8%
Enaghoughter East					
Population	139	77	11	13	9%
Houses	24	18	6	5	21%
Enaghoughter West					
Population	70	50	7	2	3%
Houses	13	7	5	1	8%
Garranes					
Population	76	63	1	1	1%
Houses	11	11	3	1	9%
Goleen					
Population	144	117	46	73	51%
Houses	26	18	46	32	123%
Gortbrack					
Population	53	38	3	2	4%
Houses	8	6	4	1	13%
Gortduff					
Population	131	79	9	9	7%
Houses	23	14	9	3	13%

	1841	1851	1997	2002	2002 as % of 1841
Gortnacarriga					
Population	110	63	20	25	23%
Houses	20	13	8	6	30%
Gortnagashel					
Population	39	16	0	20	0%
Houses	5	2	0	0	0%
Gortyowen					
Population	97	94	18	10	10%
Houses	15	16	7	4	27%
Greenane					
Population	38	16	4	5	13%
Houses	3	2	2	1	33%
Gunpoint					
Population	146	66	17	11	8%
Houses	24	6	9	4	17%
Kealfadda					
Population	230	100	13	14	6%
Houses	41	16	10	6	15%
Kilbarry					
Population	27	15	0	0	0%
Houses	3	2	0	0	0%
Kilbrown					
Population	58	35	15	16	28%
Houses	9	8	8	6	67%
Kilcomane					
Population	196	62	1	3	2%
Houses	34	10	4	2	6%
Killeane					
Population	68	30	2	1	1%
Houses	10	6	6	1	10%
Kilpatrick					
Population	78	44	0	0	0%
Houses	10	6	1	0	0%
Knock					
Population	109	39	10	12	11%
Houses	17	12	5	3	18%
Knockgallane					
Population	51	36	7	6	12%
Houses	10	6	5	2	20%

	1841	1851	1997	2002	2002 as % of 1841
Knockatassonig					
Population	0	1	0	0	
Houses	0	3	0	0	
Knockeenagearagh					
Population	65	19	1	0	0%
Houses	10	3	5	0	0%
Knockeens					
Population	123	81	12	18	15%
Houses	19	12	9	7	37%
Lackareagh					
Population	78	52	6	9	12%
Houses	12	5	3	3	25%
Lackavaun					
Population	85	66	8	5	6%
Houses	17	14	7	1	6%
Lackenakea					
Population	34	20	5	6	18%
Houses	6	4	2	2	33%
Leamcon					
Population	82	33	17	13	16%
Houses	12	7	7	5	42%
Leenane					
Population	132	52	3	3	2%
Houses	27	13	8	1	4%
Letter					
Population	134	50	15	11	8%
Houses	21	10	9	6	29%
Lissacaha					
Population	281	154	29	21	7%
Houses	41	25	20	9	22%
Lissacaha (North)					
Population	100	43	23	19	19%
Houses	14	8	10	8	57%
Lissagriffin					
Population	236	84	26	36	15%
Houses	34	16	18	11	32%
Lowertown					
Population	342	171	55	44	13%
Houses	62	29	33	14	23%

	1841	1851	1997	2002	2002 as % of 1841
Mallavoge					
Population	108	54	0	0	0%
Houses	16	14	2	0	0%
Mauladinna					
Population	90	55	2	8	9%
Houses	16	9	3	2	13%
Oughtminnee					
Population	56	38	3	7	13%
Houses	10	7	3	2	20%
Ratooragh					
Population	381	163	23	27	7%
Houses	65	29	16	10	15%
Rock Island					
Population	119	111	8	10	8%
Houses	22	24	11	5	23%
Shanavally					
Population	63	45	6	0	0%
Houses	12	12	2	0	0%
Spanishcove					
Population	80	61	3	2	3%
Houses	14	13	9	2	14%
Toor					
Population	50	32	2	2	4%
Houses	9	4	4	1	11%
Tooreen					
Population	50	12	0	0	0%
Houses	12	4	3	0	0%
Toormore					
Population	370	343	39	57	15%
Houses	73	71	41	21	29%

TOWNLAND OF TOORMORE

by Betty Barry

The townland of Toormore (*Túar-Mór*) comprising 605 acres, is situated between Schull and Goleen. It is on the road built during 1845–1846. At that time, Toormore Bridge was completed at the cost of £70. Today, heavy vehicles travel on it, which were unheard of in that era.

During 1850–1852, about 44 families lived in Toormore. They were self-supporting people who fished and grew crops on their small holdings. The women reared fowl and pigs, and they also made their own clothes, knitted socks, caps, geansays (pullovers), made their own bedclothes and patchwork quilts – worked on frames. They helped each other. In that land lived carpenters, tailors, masons and a blacksmith. There were three grocery shops. They had cows also. The men collected seaweed and sand to fertilise their crops. Near Toormore beach is the 'Palaice Strand' where pilchards, an oily fish, were cured for export.

Later, many of the young people emigrated to Canada and the United States. Some joined World War I. One, a William Donovan, lost his life on the 'world's first battle cruiser', HMS *Invincible*, which weighed 17,526 tonnes. All but six of her 1,021 crew died, including William 'Boatswain' on 6th May 1916, blown up by German naval gunfire. During the 1950s, electric power was provided for Toormore. Soon afterwards, a spring well was bored and water was piped into the homes. Electricity and water were such a gift – the quality of life improved vastly. Visitors and tourists came on holidays and enjoyed their time swimming, sight-seeing, even walking to the top of Cnoc a Phúcru, and taking photographs of the beautiful scenery. Some came with horse-drawn caravans, some cycled and brought tents. People returned and bought sites and built beautiful homes. Some live in them permanently, and others use them as holiday houses. Many people prefer to stay at bed and breakfast accommodation.

At present in Toormore there are three bed and breakfasts: 'Carraig

Goleen Past and Present 149

Mór House', run by Betty and Jim Johnson; 'Seafront', run by Margaret and George Whitley; 'Fortview Farmhouse', run by Violet and Richard Connell; and 'Altar Restaurant – Antonio's Ristorante and Pizzeria.

An old saying in Toormore was: 'If you drink a mug of Toormore water, you will certainly return for more.'

Lobster Pond, RockIsland, Goleen, Co Cork.

SALT FISH, SMUGGLERS AND SPANISH GALLEONS; THE CHEQUERED HISTORY OF CROOKHAVEN

By Joe Kerrigan

The tiny hamlet of Crookhaven lies about as far down in south-west Cork as you can go without falling into the sea, tucked snugly on the sheltered side of a narrow neck of land which creates a deep inlet – the 'crooked haven' which gave the little settlement its name. It's the very epitome of a sleep fishing village. Brightly coloured boats bob at anchor; pastel-coloured cottages slumber in the sunshine along the sloping street. A pub spill tables and chairs out on the quayside among the drying fishing nets, a small shop sells groceries and postcards, as well as shrimping nets, buckets and spades. It looks as though nothing ever has or ever could happen to disturb its peace.

Yet Crookhaven has as chequered and colourful a history as the wildest adventure story. Smuggling and shipwrecks, burnings and battles, East India merchantmen and Spanish galleons, lobsters, pichards, traders, businessmen, soldiers, spies and starving emigrants – it has known them all. This tiny settlement even played a major role in the development of world communications, and at one time was a vital link between Wall Street and London.

The principal reasons for Crookhaven's enduring importance from early times are threefold: firstly its extensive, deep, safe harbour, almost a mile in length, protected from all but the most unusual winds; secondly, that harbour's strategic location at one of the last landfall points on the Irish coast, for either the southern route to Spain, Portugal and Africa, or the western route for the New World; and thirdly, the exceptionally rich fishing grounds in the surrounding waters.

It is probable that Greek and Phoenician traders visited this coastline in ancient times. By the twelfth century, there was a church here, dedicated to St Molaggi – perhaps the same saint who gave his name to the abbey of Timoleague (Tigh Molaggi) further back along the coast towards Cork. In the sixteenth century, when England was making determined attempts to subdue her troublesome neighbour, she kept a very sharp eye on this outlying harbour, fully aware of the dangers to be feared from unfriendly countries wishing to ally themselves with the Irish rebels. It would be all too easy for a French or Spanish fighting ship to slip into Crookhaven unnoticed. In 1601, just prior to the fateful battle of Kinsale, there were constant rumours of Spanish galleons arriving at or sailing close by Crookhaven. In September of that year, Sir George Carew wrote urgently to the Privy Council:

> 'There arrived at Crookehaven [*sic*] one Captain Love who in a small pinnace recovered this coast and from thence overland came unto me. Before this can come into your hands, it is very probable that the Spaniards will make their descent in Ireland. He saw the fleet (full of land men and ensigns) stand to the northward and they are bound for this realm. He reports that most of the Irish that are in Spain are in the fleet...'

In early December, a terse message to the Queen's representative spoke of 'Spanish ships arrived a Crookhaven' but tantilisingly there are no further details on the records to confirm this. Tradition has it, however, that a Spanish ship was wrecked at Galley Cove, a rocky bay a mile or so back from the village on the seaward side of the peninsula. Shipwrecks have been an inevitable part of life here throughout history, due to the rough waters and savage rocks on this part of Ireland's coast. There is an entertaining sequel to one such: that of the *Barbara* out of Berehaven, which sank with a cargo of spirits in the harbour in 1829. A hundred and forty years later, in 1969, a diver recovered several bottles of brandy from the wreck and claimed that the contents were still drinkable.

The famed Fastnet Lighthouse was built in response to public outcry when another ship, the *Steven Whitney* was wrecked in 1847 with great loss of life. The first building was a cast-iron structure, 63 feet tall, which burned oil in its lamp, while three dwellings for the families of the light-keepers were built on Rock Island in Crookhaven Bay (which also has its own small lighthouse, as well as a Napoleonic signal tower). The iron tower, however, could not withstand the savagery of the sea, and in 1891 a new structure of Cornish granite was commissioned, to stand 176 feet tall. A shore-based headquarters was built on

Rock Island and the stone was brought out by boat. Local tradition has it that workers were paid a half-crown or two shillings and six-pence a time for rowing the heavy blocks out to the Fastnet Rock, but although the image is attractive, the work is more likley to have been done by steamer. Today, the lighthouse stands as a beacon to all pass-ing shipping, and is the focal point for the thrilling Fasnet Yacht Race held every four years.

Despite its tiny size, Crookhaven has a long history as a trading port because of its strategic position. In the seventeenth century it was list-ed, along with larger harbours like Cork, Waterford and Limerick, as being one of the principal exporters of wool, hides, yarn, hogshead staves and pipestaves. There is evidence of exotic items being import-ed in return, including ginger and other spices, as well as silks. In later centuries, large quantitities of butter, oats, wheat and pork were exported, with timber and coal being occasionally imported. Up to the nineteenth century, overland communications between Crookhaven and the rest of Ireland were extremely difficult, and goods were trans-ported onwards by coastal vessels. Partly because of this high trading profile, but also because the harbour came to be much used by the British navy and East India merchant ships as a useful stopping point on longer voyages, the isolated little village boasted customs and excise, coastguards and a police barracks. This somewhat top-heavy infrastructure was established by the British Government to protect fishing activities and prevent smuggling, as well as watching for potential coastal invasion or the infiltration of enemy spies.

Although it is difficult to prove, it is likely that a good deal of smug-gling did go on. There are several deep caves hidden under Streek Head which forms the tip of the Crookhaven peninsula, and tradition has it that these were used by illegal traders to store their precious cargoes of lace and old brandy. At a time when government strictures forbade the export of native wool, local people delighted in finding ingenious ways to get fleeces out to the waiting markets in Europe. One popular trick was to pack the wool tightly in butter casks, sealing it with a layer of the official product so that if opened, it would appear to be full of butter. On moonless nights, there would be hushed voic-es in quiet inlets from whence small boats would make their way to ships waiting out at sea. After such night-time activity, the next morn-ing might show tell-tale scraps of wool caught on thorn bushes, but seldom were the smugglers caught.

Fishing and the export of fish have always been important here. In the seventeenth century, Sir William Hull, an English tenant of the Earl of Cork, developed an industry across the harbour from the vil-

lage. In his 'Pilchard Palace' fish was salted or smoked and then bar-
relled for export. It gave useful employment to many people in the
surrounding area, but this did not stop them turning against Sir
William during the 1641 rebellion, attacking his household, burning
his property to the ground, and carrying off all his goods. The
aggrieved Sir William immediately wrote to the British Crown, listing
in detail everything he had lost with a careful valuation of each item,
including 'all the fishing sellers [cellars] which cost above £3,500'. In
later years, merchants from Brittany sailed across regularly to bargain
with local fishermen for lobster, crayfish, sea urchins, periwinkles and
salmon with which to furnish French dining tables.

In 1659, Crookhaven had just 36 inhabitants. By 1837, the population had expanded to 424 – a large number for such a small area. By
this time communications had been improved by the making of the
Skibbereen–Crookhaven road during the Famine of 1822–23, both as
a relief measure and as a public work. The population of Crookhaven
may have felt that times were improving. Then came Black '47 and a
far more terrible famine than anyone could have imagined.

The little settlement of Crookhaven was cruelly hit. There were two
soup kitchens set up there in 1847, an indication of the relief needed.
Of 91 children on the school roll in 1846, only eight remained in
March 1847. Now the position of the safe harbour as the last landfall
on the Irish coast became something of a blessing. Ships pausing
before the Atlantic crossing took off large numbers of desperate and
starving emigrants who had not the means to get to Cork. Many of
their names are lost to us; but some at least must have succeeded in
reaching the New World and a new life.

In the 1850s and 1860s there was much activity around the copper
mines which were opened on Streek and Brow Heads by speculators.
Copper has been mined in this part of West Cork on a small scale since
prehistoric times; and although the Crookhaven mines never produced very much, they would have given welcome employment to
many before they closed in the 1860s. Today evidence of their presence can still be seen on Brow Head in the ruined cottages of former
mine workers, or even in the green-streaked stones which can be
picked up everywhere.

The next two people to influence Crookhaven's history were also to
make vital use of Brow Head. Julius Reuter, who had built up his rep-
utation as a provider of news stories from across the world, decided to
set up a signal station here in 1863 from which information newly
arrived from America could be transmitted to Cork by telegraph wire
and thence to London. His staff rowed out to meet the steamers as

they arrived from their Atlantic crossing and retrieved canisters tossed overboard containing despatches from Reuter's staff. A signal tower dating from Napoleonic times was utilised as a lookout point. It was thus that the latest news from the Civil War was received in London. Since it got to Cork first, however, the *Cork Examiner* was often able to publish a 'scoop' in advance of the *London Times* – a feat which delighted its editors.

After the telegraph came the turn of radio. Guglielmo Marconi, whose mother was Irish, and who had married a daughter of the Earl of Inchiquin, decided that Crookhaven would be an excellent site for a radio station which would transfer messages from America to Englan. He accordingly set this up in 1901 in an old police barracks in the village, later moving it to Brow Head, close to the old signal tower used by Reuter. Arthur Nottage from Derbyshire was the first manager of Marconi's station; he grew to love the place and when he retired, opened a small pub in the village. His name can still be seen above the door, although 'Daddy Nottage', as he was affectionately known, has long since passed on.

The little church of St Brendan which stands on a grassy knoll above the village dates from the 1700s, but probably replaces earlier buildings. In its peaceful graveyard the grass waves long and tall around ancient stones which record losses at sea, untimely drownings or the quiet end of well-run life. This church and graveyard featured in a 1950s film, *I Thank A Fool*, starring Susan Hayward, and in O'Sullivan's pub on the quayside, faded black-and-white stills from the film (in which all the villagers appeared as extras) are still displayed with pride.

Crookhaven has always had a hypnotic, almost siren-like attraction for its visitors. Once they had discovered its sloping sunlit street, its peaceful atmosphere, its visible reminders of an historic past, they are inevitably drawn back again and again. While winter and shorter days do come, even to this favoured spot, that, according to the locals, is the best time to be here. 'We have it all to ourselves then.'

THE RAID ON THE FASTNET LIGHTHOUSE

by Frank Lannin

I was just 13 years of age when the amazing story of the Fastnet Raid was told to me. It happened during a turf-cutting session at Ardmanagh bog, which lies close to Schull. During the summer holidas I was often sent to help Charlie Cotter with the saving of hay or turf. Charlie was one of those brave men who took part in the Fastnet Raid, an event that is still talked about and marvelled at throughout West Cork. Before Charlie recalled the Fastnet Raid, he told much about the terrible conditions in the country at that time. He often referred to the 'reign of terror' which prevailed. He was scarcely 18 when he joined the Schull company of the Irish Republican Army. At that time, the Commandant of the Schull Company was a young trainee teacher at St Patrick's Training College – Sean Lehane, a native of Scairt near Bantry. Charlie described him as the bravest of the brave.

In the weeks and months prior to the Fasnet Raid, the IRA had been winning the battle against the Crown Forces. The Battle of Kilmichael was the turning point in West Cork. Many of the RIC barracks in West Cork, including Schull, had fallen to the IRA. The Sinn Féin courts were established and Republican police were on patrol. Branches of Cumann na mBan had been established all over West Cork. These were groups of dedicated women who operated an intelligence service superior to that of the enemy. In the Schull area they were trained in the art of intelligence by a young lady named Leslie Price. She spent some months in Schull and was never suspected by the police. She was later to become the wife of General Tom Barry.

As part of their strategy in West Cork, the IRA carried out attacks on lorries and armoured cars and found that the most effective weapon in such attacks were land mines. But explosives were needed and gelignite was not available. That is why the IRA turned their attention to the Fastnet Lighthouse. They knew there were large stores of explosives on the Rock. The Fastnet Raid was first mooted by

Rickie Collins. He was captain of the Goleen company and a light-keeper at the Fastnet from 1912 to 1918. Because of his knowledge of the Rock, Rickie was tipped to lead the raiding party – then came a temporary set-back. Rickie was arrested by Auxiliary Forces and jailed for terrorist offences.

At this point John O'Regan of Schull volunteered to lead the raid-ing party. John had grown up with the sea and knew every nook and cranny along the coastline from Schull to Mizen Head. The other vol-unteers selected for the raid had the utmost confidence in John's abil-ity to 'pull off' the daring escapade. In Charlie's words, 'he was cool and daring and cute as a fox'. The raid on the Fastnet was a dangerous mission. There were 47 armed Marines in Schull Coastguard Station (located near the present Garda barracks) not to mention police and military. The raid would have to be carried out in total darkness in a sea that is never very calm in the Fastnet area. Before such raids it was customary for the volunteers to go to confession. Volunteers in the Schull area were fortunate that Fr Denis Aherne, CC in Schull, was always willing to hear their confession and give them his blessing. The then Bishop of Cork, Dr Coholan, had decreed otherwise. On the evening of 28th June 1921, John O'Regan and Alex McFarlane piloted the motor boat *Golden Fort* out of Schull harbour. It was stage one of the Fastnet Raid. At Gun Point, Michael O'Donovan, captain of the Leamcon company, had assembled the other volunteers who were to form the raiding party. They were Sean Lehane, Sean O'Driscoll, Charles Cotter, Jim Hayes and Tom Hickey. At dusk the *Golden Fort* left Long Island channel and headed seaward. Very soon John O'Regan became convinced that, due to the rough conditions of the sea, it would not be possible to land that night at the Rock. Instead it was decided to land on Oilean Cleire. There Sean Lehane made the decision to postpone the raid until the following night. Leaving the others on the island, John O'Regan and Alex McFarlane brought the *Golden Fort* back to Schull so that no suspicion would be aroused by its absence. John was also anxious to establish his presence in Schull on Sunday where he attended 11 o'clock mass. That evening John left Schull, this time in the motor boat *Irene*. At Gun Point he picked up Tim Murphy, Colla, Michael Murphy, Gun Point, William Daly, Lowertown, and Michael O'Donovan. They landed on Oilean Cleire and Michael O'Donovan and Tim Murphy brought the *Irene* back to Gun Point where much work remained to be done in preparation for the landing of the spoils if the raid were successful. On Oilean Cleire, Sean Lehane had obtained a 24-foot fishing boat, *Maire Cait*, which was owned by Tadgh O'Regan. The June sun was setting as the *Maire*

Cait was steered out of North Harbour. On board were 12 men, Sean Lehane, Sean O'Driscoll, John O'Regan, Charlie Cotter, Jim Hayes, Tom Hickey, Michael Murphy, William Daly, Dan O'Driscoll, Dan Leonard, Dan Daly and Sean O'Regan. The last four were natives of the island. As dusk burned to darkness, the *Maire Cait* was on her westward journey. Then the lights of the British patrol boat appeared. They watched her circle the Fastnet and head off towards Mizen Head. They had evaded her searchlights and the countdown was beginning. The raiders reckoned that they had about three hours to complete their mission before the return of the patrol boat.

At midnight the *Maire Cait*, in total darkness, approached the Fastnet Rock. The breeze had freshened and caused the usual swell around the Rock and there was a rise and fall of several feet. The anchor was let out and and boat moved slowly to the landing place. Positioned on the bow was John O'Regan, a rope tied around his waist, a revolver in his pocket, and balancing himself with the rise and fall of the boat. He would have to select the right moment to jump on the Rock and catch the iron ring, which was fixed to the Rock. He knew where the ring was fixed, but to grasp it in total darkness was a feat that few would attempt. His vast experience as a seaman was now to be put to the test. As a wave was rising he jumped. It was a tense moment. As the wave covered him, he grasped the ring with both hands. (It was an occasion for hand clapping, but not tonight.) In seconds he had made the boat fast and the rest of the raiding party were landing on the platform. The huge steel door of the lighthouse was not locked. John was first up the spiral stairway leading to the room where the lightkeeper was on duty. He put up no resistance and, as a precaution, the wireless was dismantled. Seventeen boxes of guncotton and three boxes of detonators and primers were loaded on to the *Maire Cait* by means of the lighthouse derrick. In all, the spoils weighed but one ton. The daring mission was accomplished. At Gun Point, Michael O'Donovan and the men of Leamcon company were waiting to unload the spoils. Before dawn the 20 boxes were carefully concealed near Michael O'Donovan's house. Next night under cover of darkness, the boxes were moved in two horses and carts to a safe location at Leamcon where a bunker was prepared. All of those who took part in the Fastnet Raid have not passed from our midst – *Lúistin geal go raibh acu.* I was fortunate to know most of the members of the Fastnet raiding party and one of them, Sean O'Driscoll, also wrote the story of the raid for me some years ago. He was captain of the Ballydehob company and later became Commandant of the Seventh Battalion. His family were building contractors and built the Munster and Leinster Bank in Schull, now the AIB.

Many tributes have been paid to those men who risked all for Irish freedom. This is the tribute paid to the Schull men by Liam Deasy, author of *Towards Ireland Free*: 'They rose manfully to the demands that were made of them and gave of their best in achieving the objectives placed before them, but of recognition and appreciation for their heroic services they thought nothing. Such were the men of the Schull Battalion to whose memory I would like to pay tribute in affection and gratitude.'

Threshing the corn at the farm of Stephen Barry, Clogher 1960.

OUR PARISH

This series on the townlands of this parish is intended to indicate the decline in population caused by the Famine, and related disease and emigration; and also highlight matters of archaeological and/or historical interest. It is written weekly by Michael Raymond O'Donovan for the parish newsletter.

The Townland of Altar

Altóir means 'altar', possibly so named from the altar-shaped *cromleach* at the south side, which was probably used as a mass rock in penal times.

	Population	Houses
1841	205	36
1851	196	38
1997	5	12

Three houses are occupied, two are unoccupied and seven are holiday homes. Tenants' names in the 1850s were Johnson, King, Melvill, Allen, Donovan, Daly, Baker, Williamson, Bennett, Morris, Sullivan and Mahony. The landlord was William Baylie. Archaeological sites of interest include the Bronze Age tomb or *cromleach* mentioned at the outset, and a cave known as *pluas* at the east side. The Protestant church known as 'Teampall na mbocht' was built by Rev WA Fisher in 1847. The present rectory is adjacent to the church. The Church Education Society (Protestant) school which functioned in Famine times recorded its highest roll in 1847, when 289 attended the school. The master was Tom King. The present school closed in 1941 when 28 pupils were on the rolls. The last school master was Mr Evanson. In the nineteenth century a Daly family had a grocery shop here. In times past the post office was in this townland but was later moved to Toormore. When in the Altar, it was run in later years by the Johnson and Evanson families.

The Townland of Arderavinna

Ard Daire Fhine means the 'height of Daire Fhine'. He was an ancient chieftain. The townland is 702 acres in size.

	Population	*Houses*
1841	336	64
1851	169	30
1997	31	19

Thirteen houses are occupied, two are unoccupied and four are holiday homes. The tenants' names in the 1850s were Coughlan, Goggin, Sullivan, Collins, Johnson, McCarthy, Hunt, Wilcock, Ferguson, Gorman, Baker, King, Cotter, Reacroft, Dukelow, Doyle and Allen. The landlords were W Hull and A Cole. Arderavinna is unique in having all Catholic churches, at the east end of the parish, built in this townland. The first recorded was built circa 1731. This was a thatched structure and was replaced in 1805. When this church collapsed in 1825, it was replaced by Ballinskeagh church in 1826. The present church, Lowertown, was built in 1967. There was a mass rock at the east side of the townland but it is gone now. The first national school here (Lowertown) opened in March 1846. It had 277 pupils on the rolls, 160 boys and 117 girls; and only one teacher in the first year. After 124 years of continuous education, it closed on 30th June 1970. When the school closed it had 41 on the rolls – 20 boys and 21 girls. Lowertown Creamery, which still flourishes, was opened in 1935. Archaeological sites include a standing stone (*galán*) and a portal dolman – the only one in Mizen peninsula. There is a children's burial ground at the north side. Smithies were owned by the Wilcox family circa 1900, Driscolls in the 1910s and P Hegarty in the 1950s. A hardware shop was owned by the Ferguson family from the 1920s to the 1950s. A holiday home near the site of Ballinaskeagh church was formerly a priest's residence and later used as a medical dispensary. Nearby was a pound field. Will Joiner was a carpenter here in the early part of the last century.

The Townland of Arduslough

Árd Saileach means 'height of the willow trees'. The area of the townland is 55 acres.

	Population	*Houses*
1841	39	7
1851	34	7
1997	0	4

The four houses are holiday homes. Supple and Kelly were the only tenants in the 1850s. The landlord was Lord Clinton. Of historical and archaeological interest is a megalithic tomb (wedge grave) on the north side and at the west side is a stone with markings somewhat similar to Ogham writing, but it is not confirmed as such. A lake in the townland acts as a reservoir for Crookhaven village.

The Townland of Ballybrack

Báile Breac means 'speckled hamlet or village'. Area 121 acres.

	Population	Houses
1841	122	21
1851	70	12
1997	3	2

One house is occupied and one is unoccupied. Tenants' names in 1850s were Donovan, Gallavan, Kathegan (Cadogan), Harte, Sweetnam, Dawley (Daly) and Driscoll. The landlord was William Lewis. The smithy in Ballybrack, which was owned by John O'Sullivan, was the last smithy to operate in Goleen parish. It ceased to function in 1989.

The Townland of Ballydevlin

'Ballydevlin' derives from *beal an dileann* – 'the mouth of the flood or tide'. The area of the townland is 649 acres.

	Population	Houses
1841	462	81
1851	302	59
1997	49	49

Twenty-one houses are occupied, three are unoccupied and twenty-five are holiday homes. Tenants' names in the 1950s were Swanton, Clancy, Driscoll, Goggin, Nagle, Downey, Bohane, Mahony, Coughlan, Brown, Donovan, King, Collins, Sullivan, Lee, Murray, McCarthy, Rev John Foley, Allen and Burchill. The landlord was Lionel J Fleming. This townland is also of considerable interest historically and archaeologically. A *cromleach* or wedge tomb is seen at the south side, but is now difficult to find. The foundations of a lime kiln are near Ballydevlin strand. An O'Mahony castle was at the west side near Goleen harbour, but is now gone. Some famine graves are on a hill at the north side.

A Methodist meeting hall was built near the main road at the north side and functioned from 1889 to 1930. The foundations and steps are all that now remain. Dr McCormick had a dispensary here in Famine times and a petty sessions court functioned in the 1850s. Ballydevlin

House, the residence of the Fleming family, was for many years the residence of the parish priest. A Church of Ireland school was in use here in pre-Famine times. The highest number of pupils recorded was 177 in 1848. The last Church of Ireland school closed in 1968–9 when seven pupils were on the rolls. The last teacher was Ms O'Neill. Trades and tradesmen, early in the nineteenth century, were: Andy Donovan, weaver; a boat builder whose name is now unknown; McCarthys, who were smiths; Downey was a shoemaker; Loves had a grocery shop and Hurleys had a store where farm produce was purchased. There was a pound field in the townland in the 1840s. In the 1821 townlands list, Ballydevlin was divided into four townlands: Ballydevlin, Ballydevlin East, Ballydevlin Middle and Ballydevlin West.

The Townland of Ballynaule

Beal an Shail means 'mouth or opening of salt water'. The area of the townland is 91 acres.

	Population	Houses
1841	27	4
1851	31	4
1997	2	2

One house is residential and one is a holiday home. Instead of the expected decline of 40% to 50%, this townland shows a slight increase in population from 1841 to 1851. This was possibly due to people moving nearer to where soup kitchens operated, and staying in some cabins vacated by the dead; there was little to return to. Tenants' names in the 1850s were Carty, Daly, Coughlan, Mahony, Driscoll and the Brow Head Mining Company. The landlord was Lord Clinton. Early in the nineteenth century a grain store was sited near the cockle strand. Fish palaces (used to process pilchards) were also here in the seventeenth century. The townland has some sandy beaches and a caravan park at Galley Cove.

The Townland of Ballyrisode

Ballyrisode, sometimes pronounced Ballyrizzard, is possibly from *baile an disert* meaning 'place of retreat'. Its area is 591 acres.

	Population	Houses
1841	371	73
1851	141	27
1997	39	25

Eleven houses are occupied, one is unoccupied and twelve are holiday homes. One is a recently built coffee and gift shop. Tenants' names in the 1850s were Donovan, Cunningham, Hegarty, Allen, Johnson, Boyle, Kingston, Melville, Coursey, White and Coughlan.

The landlord was Richard B Hungerford. Part of the west side of the townland is known as Coom. Ballyrisode has much of archaeological and historical interest. In the White Strand are a number of grave stones, possibly marking the graves of seamen whose bodies were washed ashore. At the south side is a large burial ground, now disused, and nearby is a large souterrain. A small *cill* is also at the north side near the main road. In the forest at the north side is a megalithic tomb (wedge grave). Pre-history mines are also here where some axes were discovered in the early part of the last century. The foundation stone of the Rev Stoney Memorial Hall are near the main road at the north side. This was a Church of Ireland place of worship from 1900 to 1959. Ballyrisode House, recently restored, was the home of the Hungerford family.

The Townland of Ballyvogue Beg

The small habitation of O'Bogue. The area of the townland is 100 acres.

	Population	Houses
1841	55	9
1851	21	3
1997	5	1

Two houses are occupied and there is one holiday home. Tenants' names in the 1850s were Connor, Downey and Base. The landlord was John Hyde. Near the main road is a large megalithic tomb of a type known as a wedge grave. This tomb is now in a ruinous state. Additional information to hand says that the grocery shop in Ballyvogue Mor was owned by Mary O'Brien.

The Townland of Ballyvogue Mor

Baile Ui Bhuadhaig Mór means the 'large habitation of O'Bogue'. The area of the townland is 240 acres.

	Population	Houses
1841	83	12
1851	53	7
1997	11	10

Six houses are occupied, one is unoccupied and three are holiday homes. Tenants' names in the 1850s were Donovan, Leary, Driscoll, Carty and Cullinane. The landlord was Henry E Warren. At the north side of the townland is a ring fort, and at the west side, near the main road, was a single standing stone, now fallen. These stones, when not part of an alignment long gone, are possibly the grass markers of an ancient chieftain or a territorial boundary marker of ancient times. A souterrain (underground passage) is also in the townland. Cullinanes had a forge here in the mid-1800s. In this forge the drill tips used in the copper mines in the Mizen area were honed and sharpened. A grocery shop served the townland in the nineteenth century; the owner's name is now forgotten.

The Townland of Ballyvonane

Baile Fionnáin means 'Fionnáin's house or habitation'. The area is 238 acres.

	Population	Houses
1841	82	13
1851	37	6
1997	0	7

Five are holiday homes and two houses are unoccupied. Tenants' names in the 1850s were Goggin, Raecroft, Driscoll, McCarthy and Twomey. The landlords were James O'Callaghan and the Earl of Bandon. Part of this townland was known as Scart. A stone cairn is at the north side near Trá Lárgagh.

The Townland of Balteen

'Balteen' comes from the Gaelic *bailtín*, meaning 'a small holding'. It was formerly known as Bailtín MacCraith.

	Population	Houses
1841	59	12
1851	30	4
1997	3	2

One house is occupied and one is unoccupied. The tenants' names in the 1850s were Sullivan, Daly, Cowhig and Luacy. The landlord was W Hull. Some 19th-century copper mineshafts are present here.

The Townland of Balteen (Goleen)

Bailtín means a 'little hamlet'. It is 629 acres in area.

	Population	Houses
1841	187	32
1851	114	23
1997	14	14

Seven houses are occupied, one is unoccupied and six are holiday homes. Tenants' names in the 1850s were Coughlan, Neill, Mahony, Sullivan, Carty, Sheehan, Leary, Connell, Driscoll, Harrington and Mullins. The landlord was Thomas Clarke. In a field in the townland known as Gort an tSagart is a large flat-topped rock where mass was offered in penal times. Some rock art in the form of circular cup marks is on some glacial erratics in the townland. Some Famine graves can still be identified in this area. A ring fort is at the north side overlooking Dunmanus Bay. A Coughlan family had a grocery shop here in the 1930s, and earlier in the century a Harrington family had a smithy in the townland.

The Townland of Barnatonicane

Bearna an Tonacáin means 'gap of the slippery place'. The area is 263 acres.

	Population	Houses
1841	128	20
1851	34	6
1997	7	4

Three houses are occupied and one is unoccupied. Names of tenants who were in occupation in the 1850s were McCarthy, Cronin, Evans and James O'Callaghan. The landlords were James O'Callaghan and the Earl of Bandon, who owned 245 acres. Cill Cheangail cemetery and medieval church ruin are at the southside. Outside the cemetery on the river bank is a *baulán* stone. Rock Cottage was the home of the landlord James O'Callaghan and is at the east side.

The Townland of Beakeen

Beicín means 'small field or haggard'. It has an area of 99 acres.

	Population	Houses
1841	86	12
1851	30	5
1997	6	5

Three houses are occupied full time and two are holiday homes. The tenants' names in the 1850s were Hayes, Reacroft, Callaghan and Donovan. The landlord was William Lewis. The *galán* (standing stone) that stood at the west end of the townland is now gone.

The Townland of Boulysallagh

This name means 'a willow enclosure', possibly where cattle were enclosed. The area of the townland is 252 acres.

	Population	*Houses*
1841	100	18
1851	81	17
1997	20	30

Eight houses are residential and 22 are holiday homes. Tenants' names in the 1850s were Coughlan, Donovan, Cammier, Driscoll, Mahony, Griffin, Lamb, Scully, Nolan, Sullivan, Crowley and Hegarty. The landlord was Margaret Notter. In 1852 a company was set up to prospect for copper in the townland. This company, in common with other prospecting companies of that time, proved a scam. However, during prospecting, an ancient pre-history (1500–1100 BC) copper mine was discovered with some mining mauls still in place.

The early eighteenth century RC church was in this townland; hence the name Bothar an tSeipeil, on the old road that led to the church. This church was later replaced by another, built where the curate's house stood. There is a small *cill* at the north side of the townland. Dan and Jack O'Sullivan had a forge in the 1930s–1960s and Dan O'Connor had a small grocery. A Hamilton had a milling business for a short period. Goleen parish hall and national school (both recently renovated) are also in Boulysallagh. At present, 39 pupils are on the roll book. Ms Margaret Lannin and Ms Kathleen Crowley are currently the teachers. The first national schools were opened by Fr Foley, PP 1848–1855), in 1849. Two schools, one male and one female, were then in Goleen. The boys' school had 71 pupils on the rolls and the girls' school had 82.

The Townland of Caher

Cathair means 'stone fort'. The area of the townland is 466 acres.

	Population	*Houses*
1841	194	34
1851	74	14
1997	16	8

Five houses are residential, two are unoccupied and one is a holiday home. Tenants' names in the 1850s were Mahony, Peer, Hurley, Leary, Coughlan, Downey, Barry and Reilly. The landlord was Donal Leahy. There is now no trace of the stone fort that was discovered in the townland.

A souterrain (an undergound passage) was discovered here some years ago. In a rock at the top of Caher hill is a footprint which local lore says was made by a priest fleeing from pursuing redcoats. This place is known as the 'Priest's Leap'. A small well at this place is said to have properties to cure warts. In graves at the west side are the remains of sailors whose bodies were washed ashore in the distant past. Also at the west side is a sheltered *cuas*, which was used as a refuge by the local IRA unit during the War of Independence.

The Townland of Caheriverane

The name comes from the Irish *Cathair Ui Bhearain*, meaning Ui Bhearain's – Barron's – stone fort.

	Population	Houses
1841	65	13
1851	37	5
1997	11	5

There are four houses occupied now and one unoccupied. The names in the Griffiths Valuation list of the 1850s were Attridge, Allen, Evans, Donoghue and Mahony. The name Forde also occurred in the nineteenth century, but is now unknown here.

The Townland of Caherolickane

Cathair Leicne means 'stone fort'. The area is 240 acres.

	Population	Houses
1841	146	26
1851	35	15
1997	6	5

Three houses are occupied, one is unoccupied and one is a holiday home. Tenants' names in the 1850s were Moss, Minihane, Sullivan, Coughlan, Connor and Harrington. The landlords were W Baldwin and A O'Driscoll. A tailor named Minihane worked here in 1850. The rural shop which functioned in the 1940s–1950s was owned by the Moynihane family.

The Townland of Cannawee
Ceann a Mhuige means 'head of the plain'. Its area is 114 acres.

	Population	*Houses*
1841	96	16
1851	36	8
1997	15	10

Four houses are residential, six are holiday homes. According to Griffiths Valuation, tenants' names in the 1850s were Mehigan, Regan, Barry, Sheehan and Downey. The landlord was John Hyde. Sheehans had a grocery business here in the early part of the last century. Barleycove Hotel and holiday villas are also in this townland. The adjoining sandy beaches are the most popular in West Cork.

The Townland of Carrigacat and Mileen
Carrig a'Chait means the 'rock of the cats' – possibly wild. *Millín* means a 'small knoll'. These two townlands are now listed together but in the records of 1822 they are mentioned separately. The joint acreage is 838 acres.

	Population	*Houses*
1841	289	48
1851	106	24
1997	11	15

Four houses are occupied, three are unoccupied and eight are holiday homes. Tenants' names in the 1850s were Cullinane, Donovan, Carty, Brien, Regan, Holohan, Allen, Really, Sheehan, Sullivan, Driscoll, Hurley, Thomas, Harris, and the Durode Mining Company. The landlord was Lionel J Fleming.

The north side of the townland is known as Durode from *dubh fhód* meaning black sod. This area was the scene of intense mining activity in the 1840s when up to 950 tons of copper ore was raised. Due to the Famine, the mines were closed in 1847. The circular magazine that stored the explosives used in mining is almost intact. Some of the mineshafts in the area are extremely dangerous. At the north side of the main road is a raised circular area of uncertain origin.

The Townland of Carrigacurriheen
Carraig a'Churraichín means 'rock of the little swamp or marsh'. The area of the townland is 235 acres.

	Population	Houses
1841	60	10
1851	26	4
1997	0	1

The one house is unoccupied. Tenants' names in the 1850s were Regan, Simmons, Mahony, Rev Fisher, Daly and Love. The landlord was the Rev T O'Grady. The archaeological survey (1992) records some ancient huts in the townland.

The Townland of Carrigeengour

Carraigín Gabhar means the 'rock of light scad' or 'rock of the goat'. The area of the townland is 132 acres.

	Population	Houses
1841	48	8
1851	30	4
1997	7	2

Both houses are occupied. Tenants' names in the 1850s were Hegarty, Johnson, Wall and Hall. The landlord was the Rev T O'Grady. Dinny Brown was a well-known raconteur and carpenter in the townland in the 1940s–1960s.

The Townland of Carrigmanus

Carraig Maghnuis means 'rock of Manus'. The area of the townland is 78 acres.

	Population	Houses
1841	54	7
1851	16	2
1997	19	5

Four houses are occupied and one is a holiday home. Tenants' names in the 1850s were Hegarty, Summin, Regan and Glavin. The landlord was Rev T O'Grady.

Part of the townland was known as Ship. In the 1822 list of parish townlands, Ship was a separate townland; there are various local interpretations of this name.

In a field in the townland is the grave of an O'Donoghue – the last clan to occupy Dunlough Castle. The O'Neill family had a grocery shop here which functioned up to the 1980s.

The Townland of Cashelfean

Caiseal Liadhain means the 'stone fort of Liadhain'. Local tradition suggests this was the birthplace of Liadan, mother of St Kieran. The area of the townland is 1,002 acres.

	Population	*Houses*
1841	379	74
1851	128	30
1997	26	16

Eight houses are occupied, three are unoccupied and five are holiday homes. Tenants' names in the 1850s were Daly, Sweeney, Mahony, Houlahan, Wright, Shea, Kissane, Sullivan, Levis, Kingston, Pyburn, Hegarty, Brooks, Gay, Driscoll, Reacroft and Bohane. The landlords were Morgan Sullivan, William Blasby and Rev Charles Donovan.

An old disused burial ground is at the north side. An unusual feature of this *cill* is the number of graves covered with large flat stones. According to local tradition, this burial ground was used in Famine times. Kileenagh fort is at the west side. This suggests that a *cill* may have been in the fort in past times, but no trace of this exists now. At the south side is a holy well, which is now difficult to identify.

Kilthomane National School is in the townland of Cashelfean. This school, which was built in 1909, closed on 14th December 1944. On closure it had 14 on the rolls – eight girls and six boys. The first national school here was built in 1849 by Fr Foley, PP. A Church Education Society school (Protestant) which opened in Famine times had a roll of 145 pupils in 1847. This latter school closed down in 1849 when the national school opened.

A man by the name of Murray had a smithy here in the nineteenth century. The hill at the east side is known locally as Cain Hill; the old name was Knockaughna Arbutus Hill. The hill was the scene of a crash of a German bomber during World War II. There was one survivor.

The Townland of Castlemehigan

The Irish version of this name is *Casilean Ui Mhaothhagain* or 'Mehigan's castle'. The area of the townland is 118 acres.

	Population	*Houses*
1841	88	15
1851	42	8
1997	5	6

Three houses are residential and three are holiday homes. Tenants' names in the 1850s were Daly, Gleeson, Barry, Downey, Driscoll and Sullivan. The landlord was Lord Clinton. The castle that gave the townland its name was built in the fourteenth/fifteenth century by the O'Mahonys and granted to the O'Mehigans, who were bardic families to the O'Mahony clan. The castle, which was at the south side of the townland, was intact in AD 1700, but no trace now remains. There are many places of historical and archaeological importance in the townland. Some Famine graves are at the north side. A large decorated stone with cup marks and circles is also at the north side. This stone was possibly used as a mass rock in penal times. Further east is the lake which supplies water to Goleen. Several ruined houses are at the south side (some of these are now being restored). These are possibly the remains of an old fishing village. Nearby in a terraced area, a large souterrain (underground passage) was recently discovered. Possibly much of the history of this townland is still to be uncovered. A forge was in use in the nineteenth century – the name of the smith is now unknown.

The Townland of Castlepoint

The old name of most of this townland was Laharan. This was derived from *leath – fhearann* – half a *fearann*. *Fearann* is an old land measure. The present townland is 85 acres in size.

	Population	Houses
1841	45	5
1851	16	3
1997	4	3

Two houses are occupied. One is a holiday home. Names occurring in the Griffiths Valuation list in the 1850s were Mahony, Kingston, McCarthy and Driscoll. The landlord was William Levis. A 15th-century castle (Leamcon Castle) stands at the end of the peninsula on the site of a promontory fort. Nearby is an old mineshaft, possibly prehistory. The holy well, known as 'Tobarbrendán', is on the old road to the castle. Rounds were made to this well up to the 1930s. A small pier is at the north side.

The Townland of Clogher

Clochar means 'stony place or a stone ruin'. At 33 acres this is the smallest townland in the parish.

	Population	Houses
1841	13	1
1851	10	1
1997	8	3

Cornelius Coughlan was the only tenant name listed in the 1850s. The landlord was Rev T O'Grady. Downey's had a grocery shop here up to the late 1960s.

The Townland of Cloughanalehid

Clochán a Leathid means 'wide stony place'. The area is 114 acres.

	Population	Houses
1841	46	6
1851	7	1
1997	0	1

The one house is a holiday home. Only one tenant, Timothy Cullinane, is listed as an occupier in 1850. The landlord was Capain Philip Somerville. The highest point, Cnoc na Madraí (hill of the dogs, or possibly *madraí rua* – foxes), is in this in this townland. At 1,034 feet, it is the highest elevation in the parish.

The Townland of Cloughane

Clocháin means 'stone ruin or stoney place'. The area of the townland is 293 acres.

	Population	Houses
1841	100	13
1851	48	7
1997	0	3

The three houses are holiday homes. Tenants' names in the 1850s were Collins, Donovan, Downey and Hall. The landlord was Thomas Nicholls. At the west end is the Mizen Head, the most south-west point in Ireland. This is on Cloughan Island, which in past times was known as 'Oilean a'Bhioráin' – island of the point or peak. The fog signal station on the island (now part of the Mizen Vision interpretive station) was built in 1909–10 and the lighthouse was added in 1959. The suspension bridge, built in 1908–10, which links the island to the mainland, was then a feat of engineering skill. There is a small pier on the south side where the material used on the construction of the Mizen station was landed. At the north side is a 19th-century signal tower built in 1803–4. This was part of the coastal defence system built when a French invasion seemed imminent. This tower was used as a coastguard station in the 1940s. Some 19th-century copper mines are in the townland. A small circular enclosure of uncertain origin is near the Mizen roadway.

The Townland of Cloughanekilleen

Clochan a'Chillin means 'stony area of the little church'. The area of the townland is 627 acres.

	Population	Houses
1841	187	31
1851	114	22
1997	28	14

Eleven houses are occupied and three are holiday homes. Tenants' names in the 1850s were Driscoll, Sheehan, Cammier, Grimes, Barry, Donovan, Reilly, Coughlan and Goggin. The landlord was Lionel J Fleming. This townland has much of historical and archaeological interest. On a stream at the west side is a *fulacht fiadh* (an ancient cooking place); its stone-lined trough is in near-perfect condition. At the north side is a small fort. Near the south side is a raised fort enclosure with a standing stone at the west side. A small *cill* (burial ground) is in a field at the north side of the main road. A pound field was in use in the townland in the nineteenth century, where cattled seized for rent payment were held. A number of grocery shops served the area in past times: Minihane's in the nineteenth century; O'Driscoll's in the early part of the last century; and Sheehan's had a grocery business in the 1950s. A blacksmith worked here in the last century and the townland also had its *shebeen*, but the owners' names are now forgotten.

The Townland of Colleras Eighter

The name means 'lower marsh woodland'. The area is 170 acres.

	Population	Houses
1841	128	25
1851	85	18
1997	37	23

Fourteen houses are occupied, one is unoccupied and eight are holiday homes. Tenants' names in the 1850s were Cullinane, Bohane, Connor, Kelly, Barnane, Sullivan, Murphy, Jermyn, Driscoll, Collins, Regan, Carty, Mahony and Crowley. Alicia Maria Notter was the landlord. Goleen Garda Station and the old dispensary are in this townland. The large house known as Cape View was once the home of Dr McCormack, who served in this parish in Famine times.

The Townland of Colleras Oughter

Colleras Oughter means 'upper marsh woodland'. The area of the townland is 500 acres.

	Population	Houses
1841	263	49
1851	131	27
1997	7	8

Four houses are residential, one is vacant and three are holiday homes. Tenants' names in the 1850s were Notter, O'Mahony, Regan, Hegarty, Sullivan, Neville, Donovan, Driscoll, Nagle, Daly, Lamb, Coakley, Burchill and Wilbank. Florence McCarthy and Mrs Clarke were joint owners of the townland. The west side of the townland is known as Lakelands. Also at the west end, near the road, a *fulacht fiadh* was discovered some years ago; unfortunately this is now demolished.

On the old rock known as Bothar an tSean Sheipeil (the old chapel road) is a mass rock and a holy well known as Tobaranvoher, where rounds were formerly made on 2nd June, Feast of St Eoin. A pre-history copper mine, 1100–1300 BC, is in the townland. Jim Sullivan was both boatbuilder and carpenter in the townland in the early part of the last century.

The Townland of Coomfarna

Cum Fearan means a 'recess of alder trees'. It is 284 acres.

	Population	Houses
1841	12	2
1851	10	2
1997	2	1

The one house is occupied. Tenants' names in the 1850s were Minihane, Hickey, Luacey and Ellis. The landlords were W Baldwin and A O'Driscoll.

The Townland of Corelacka

Cuar Leaca means 'round or curved hillside'. The area of the townland is 309 acres.

	Population	Houses
1841	138	22
1851	87	15
1997	20	6

Four houses are occupied, one is unoccupied and one is a holiday home. Tenants' names in the 1850s were Sullivan, Daly, Coughlan, Cullinane and Peer. Three landlords jointly owned the townland. They were George Long, Margaret Notter and the representatives of Samuel Levis. A large ring fort near the east side is known as Caherbhán – 'the white fort'. This fort has a number of quartz stones.

The Townland of Corran Beg

Carn Beag means 'little cairn'. The area of the townland is 162 acres.

	Population	Houses
1841	81	12
1851	48	9
1997	4	6

Two houses are residential and four are holiday homes. Tenants' names in the 1850s were Mahony, Mehigan, Driscoll and Downey. Donal Leahy was the landlord. The hilltop on the north side is known as Stoukeen.

The Townland of Corran More

Carn Mor means 'great cairn'. In past times this townland was known as Carn Ui Ghlaimhín, or Glavin's Cairn. The area of the townland is 173 acres.

	Population	Houses
1841	146	24
1851	53	8
1997	11	11

Five houses are residential and six are holiday homes. Tenants' names in the 1850s were Downey, Canty, Sullivan and Donovan. The landlord was Henry E Warren. A ring fort was in the townland, but was destroyed during road-making operations in the distant past. There is a pier at the south side. A Barry family had a tailoring business here early in the last century. The townland has links with the *Lusitania*, which was torpedoed off the Old Head of Kinsale during World War I. A young boy who survived the sinking often stayed in

Corran More with his aunt, a Coughlan lady. In later years, he joined the priesthood and was ordained as Fr Conleth of the Franciscan Order.

The Townland of Cove

Cobh is an Irish word meaning 'sea-inlet'. The townland is 283 acres in size.

	Population	Houses
1841	254	49
1851	53	10
1997	13	7

Six houses are occupied and one is a holiday home. Surnames at the time of Griffiths Valuation list in the 1850s were Raecroft, Sweetnam, Kinningam, Barry, Carty and Cole. The landlord was W Hull. Cove House was the home of the landlord's agent, Luke Sweetnam. At the east side is a burial ground which has the characteristics of an early christian site. In Cove strand are the ruins of an old lime kiln. Some house ruins in the townland possibly date from Famine times. A Church Education Society school functioned here in the late 1840s. The teacher was Daniel Cole. A rural shop owned by the Roycroft family flourished up to the 1960s.

The Townland of Crookhaven

An Cruachan means 'the small hill or mound'. The modern name means 'the haven of the *cruach*'. In ancient times, the harbour was known as Cuan Deide or Deady's harbour. The area of the townland is 268 acres. The following figures refer to the joint population of the town and townland:

	Population	Houses
1841	472	97
1851	404	79
1997	39	72

Sixteen houses are residential and 56 are holiday homes. Tenants' names in the 1850s were Mahony, Rev Fisher (church and graveyard), Driscoll, Notter, Monk, Crookhaven Mining Company, Thomas, Shea, Buckley, Shaughnessy, Regan, Blake, Supple, Glavin, Leary, Ellis, Breasley, Meade, Donohoe, Cunningham, Leahy, Penrose, Donovan, Neagle, Harrington, Mullins, Matthews, Cadogan, Daly, Karney, Evans and Doyle. David Cagney was the landlord, but Issac Notter had considerable house property in the town.

Many historical events of the past are linked to Crookhaven. An O'Mahony castle was built here in the fifteenth century, but no trace of this now remains. William Jull, Boyle and Poper (who introduced several English families to Crookhaven) developed the pilchard fishing industry in the town in the mid-seventeenth century. This industry flourished for some time but was destroyed by the O'Mahonys when they sacked the town in reprisal for the confiscation of their lands by Hull. There are now remains of a star-shaped fort at the east side. A pilotage tower, similar to the two on Rock Island, was in Crookhaven. This was a ruin when surveyed in 1902 and no trace of it now exists.

Extensive copper mining was carried out in the nineteenth century. The magazines used to store the powder can still be seen, one in near-perfect condition. Some remains of the engine house and base of the chimney stack also remain.

Prior to moving to Brow Head, Marconi had his first wireless transmitting station to the rear of the present Marconi House in 1901. In past times, Crookhaven, because of it location between the old and the new world, and its sheltered and safe anchorage, was a hive of maritime activity. This activity possible peaked in the early part of the last century, during World War I, when Lloyd's and Reuters news agency had installations here in addition to the Marconi station. This made Crookhaven the news centre of the world.

A Church of Ireland school functioned here from 1847 to 1852. Forty-two pupils were on the rolls in 1847. A national school (Catholic) opened in 1848, when eight pupils were on the rolls. Susanne Bowler was the last teacher. In 1699–1700 the ruins of a church were at the west side. St Brendan's Church (Protestant), recently renovated, now stands on this site.

In the 1850s, stores (shops) in Crookhaven were owned by Monks, Noonan, Blake and Leahy; and a smithy (forge) was owned by Donal Driscoll. The commerical life of Crookhaven today revolves around the O'Sullivan family, who also run the post office. Previous people who ran this post office were Hannah O'Driscoll, Gertrude Coughlan and Florence McCarthy.

To the south of Crookhaven is the district known as Yokane. Smaller areas there are known as Monks and Blackpool.

The Townland of Derryfunction

Doire Fuinnsean means 'ash grove'. Its area is 242 acres.

	Population	Houses
1841	114	19
1851	36	6
1997	1	5

One house is occupied, one is unoccupied and three are holiday homes. Tenants' names in the townland in the 1850s were Hegarty, Nugent, Barry, Cronin and McCarthy. The landlord was J Connelly. There are old Brytes mines at the east side. A *fulacht fiadh*, or ancient cooking place is also in the townland. A rural shop which flourished in the 1940s–1950s was owned by the Nugents.

The Townland of Derryleary

'Derryleary' comes from *doire Uí Laoghaire*, 'O'Leary's oak wood'. It has an area of 183 acres.

	Population	Houses
1841	192	34
1851	73	14
1997	26	7

All seven houses are occupied. The tenants' names in the 1850s were Reacroft, Walsh, Donovan, Holland, Carthy, Minihane, Driscoll and Mahony. The landlord was W Hull. The archaeological sites here include an Iron Age fort and 19th-century copper mines. Daniel Donovan had a smithy here in the 1850s.

The Townland of Dough

Dumhach means 'sand hill of sand banks'. The area of the townland is 244 acres.

	Population	Houses
1841	87	14
1851	29	6
1997	1	5

One house is occupied, one is unoccupied and three are holiday homes. Tenants' names in the 1850s were Coughlan, Mehigan, Barry, Downey and King. The landlord was Henry E Warren. Items of archaeological and historical importance include a large standing stone. These stones may have been part of a stone alignment, an ancient boundary marker or a place where a clan leader was slain or buried.

At the south side is a place known as 'Esk an Aifreann', where possibly mass was celebrated in penal times. At the west side are some beautiful beaches and sand dunes; a mecca for tourists in summer time. The dunes are home to many species of rare plants and flowers. Also at the west side is Chimney Cove, so named from a small chimney-shaped rock off Chimney Point, which is also a blow-hole.

The Townland of Drinane

Draighneán means 'blackthorn', which abounds in the area.

	Population	*Houses*
1841	94	16
1851	60	12
1997	13	10

Four houses are occupied full time; six are holiday homes. Tenants' names in 1850 were Donoghue, Mahony, Sweetnam, McCarthy and Lannon. The landlord was W Hull. A large complex of underground passageways was discovered in this townland recently. A pound field was in use here in the 1840s. This is where the cattle, impounded by the sheriff, were kept to meet rent payments. At the south side was a small sheepfold. It no longer exists.

At the east side is an unfinished section of a Famine relief roadway. Possible the only rural drapery shop in the parish functioned here in the 1940s. It belonged to an O'Mahony family. A grocery shop also owned by the O'Mahony family operated here at the end of the nineteenth century. A carpenter's shop at the west side was owned by Jim Sweetnam. A hedge school functioned here in the nineteenth century; the master was an O'Mahony.

The Townland of Drishane

Drisean means 'place of brambles or briars'. Its area is 329 acres.

	Population	*Houses*
1841	181	27
1851	120	24
1997	20	3

Eight houses are occupied, two are unoccupied and four are holiday homes. Tenants' names in the 1850s were Neill, Hegarty, Minihane, Levis, Hellen, Young, Ryan, McCarthy, Scofield, Murray, Dawley and Harnett. The landlord was D McCarthy. Traces of an old fish palace can be seen in Drishane strand. These palaces date from the seventeenth century and were used to process pilchards, which were in plentiful supply at that time.

The Townland of Dunkelly East

Dun Cheallaigh means 'Ceallach's fortress'. The area of the townland is 290 acres.

	Population	Houses
1841	199	35
1851	32	5
1997	10	6

Four houses are occupied and two are holiday homes. Tenants' names in the 1850s were Downey, Hickey, Coughlan, Lucey, Holland and Mahony. The landlord was John Beale. The promontary fort from which the townland derives its name is on the east side. Though partially eroded by the sea, the section which remains is reasonably intact. This fortress has an underground chamber.

The Townland of Dunkelly Middle

The area of this townland is 124 acres.

	Population	Houses
1841	126	25
1851	40	10
1997	4	4

Two houses are occupied, one is unoccupied and one is a holiday home. Tenants' names in the 1850s were Fleming and Harnett. The landlord was Mr Levis. This townland was known as Poundland. At the south side is 'Cnoc a'Phuca', where a cross was erected on the summit as part of the Holy Year celebration in 1950. Some years later the cross was struck by lightning and has since fallen.

The Townland of Dunkelly West

The area of this townland is 380 acres.

	Population	Houses
1841	95	17
1851	75	15
1997	6	13

Four houses are occupied, three are unoccupied and six are holiday homes. Tenants' names in the 1850s were Donovan, Harnett, Sullivan, Collins, Kelly, Neville and McCarthy. The landlord was John Beale and Mr Uniake. Part of Dunkelly West was known as Priestland, which suggests a priest resided there in past times.

A school was opened here by Fr Foley in 1849. The highest number of pupils recorded was 82 in 1850. John Collins taught in the school in its early years. An O'Mahony castle is reputed to have been in the townland, but no evidence of this exists now. Canty's Cove at the north side was a hive of industry in the heyday of seine fishing early in the century.

At the north side of the cove, in 'Cuas an Staighre', are the pirate steps. Near the east side is a disused *cill* or burial ground. A Long family had a grocery shop here early in the century, and a carpentry shop was owned by a Collins family.

The Townland of Dunlough

Dún a Locha means 'fort or fortress of the lake'. The area of the townland is 319 acres.

	Population	Houses
1841	67	9
1851	52	9
1997	4	2

Tenants' names in the 1850s were Sheehan, Leary and Coughlan. The landlord was the Rev T O'Grady. The first O'Mahony castle built on the Mizen peninsula was built at Dunlough, on the site of an old *dún* or headland fort. This 14th/15th-century castle is an imposing structure with its flanking towers and curtain walls extending to the lake.

At the south east of the townland is 'Cuas na Naomh' where mass was celebrated in penal times. The letters I H S are carved on the rock-face. Also in the *cuas* is a holy well known as 'Tobar na Naomh', where, according to tradition, cures for mental ailments were obtained. Rounds were held here in past times. Unfortunately, due to coastal erosion, the holy well is now badly damaged.

Some other names in this place indicate a strong religious tradition in ancient times. Colomane's Cuas and Colomane's rock had possible links with St Colman, who had a church at Colomane in the parish of Caheragh. 'Carrig na hEaglish' – was there a small church or oratory here in early christian times? A field nearby is known as 'Gort na

Cille'; obviously a burial ground was here but no trace of it now exists. Also in Dunlough is a small pier and slipway, which was in use in the 1920s–1940s. A rusty winch near the slipway is a reminder of past activities. 'Cuas an Caislean' is nearby, where a small castle or outpost once stood on the cliff edge.

A Church of Ireland school opened in the townland in Famine times. Seventy-eight pupils were on the rolls in 1847. A Sheehan family had a shoemaker shop in Dunlough early in the last century.

The Townland of Dunmanus East

Dún Maghnuis means 'fortress or headland fort of Manus'. The area of the townland is 574 acres.

	Population	Houses
1841	460	81
1851	165	33
1997	14	9

Four houses are occupied and five are unoccupied. Tenants' names in the 1850s were Kingston, Donovan, Neill, Lucey, Downey, Helen, Sheahan, Daly, Sullivan, Mahony, Condon, Haulahan, Driscoll, Carty, Brown, Regan, Hoolihan, Brien, Geaney, McCarthy, Hegarty, McGrath and Meade. The landlords were Patience Noble and Rev Edward Faircho. The east side of the townland is called Moulassa (the mound of the fort), which still stands. Part of the south side is known as Tooreen – a small bleach area.

Dunmanus National School is at the east side. This school opened in 1899 and closed in June 1993. At closure it had seven pupils on the rolls. Mrs O'Sullivan, née Kingston, was the last teacher. A Protestant school functioned here from 1849 to 1852. The highest number of pupils on the rolls was 38 in 1849. Local tradition says a hedge school was in Moulassa in pre-Famine times.

Of archaeological interest is a 'boulder burial' in the estuary of Dunmanus Bay. This type of Bronze Age tomb is peculiar to the south west. Also in the estuary is a small circle of uncertain origin. The Hegarty family owned a smithy, which closed in the late 1820s. They also had a rural shop for a short period. At the east side (Coles Cross), Nugents had a shop which closed in the late 1960s.

The Townland of Dunmanus West

Dún Maghnuis means 'fortress of Manus'. The area of the townland is 574 acres.

	Population	*Houses*
1841	424	83
1851	152	28
1997	20	15

Eight houses are occupied, one is unoccupied and six are holiday homes. Tenants' names in the 1850s were Driscoll, Hodnett, Carty, Sullivan, Long, Rev W Warren, McGrath, Wilcock, Goggin, Martin, Denis, Hosford, Coady, Donovan, Butler, Dawley and Coughlan. The landlord was Patience Noble. Various parts of the townland had their own local district names. At the south side is Drinane, at the west is Cummer an Scrawn, and near the centre is Faun Mor and Skouke. Dunmanus Castle, in this townland, is the largest of the O'Mahony castles in the Mizen peninsula. Built in the fifteenth century by Donogh Mor, it holds a commanding position overlooking the bay. On the hillside near the south is a 'fallen' standing stone. At the west are a number of 19th-century mineshafts. Also here is 'Tobar na Sul' (a holy well) where cures for eye ailments were effected in times past.

The Townland of Enoughter East

Enaghoughter comes from *Eanagh Uachtar* meaning 'upper marsh'. The area of the townland is 261 acres.

	Population	*Houses*
1841	139	24
1851	77	18
1997	11	6

Five houses are occupied and one is unoccupied. Tenants' names in the 1850s were Love, Daly, Brown, Cotter, Connell and Driscoll. The landlord was J Hickson. The Wilkinson family had a grocery shop here at the end of the nineteenth century. Longs also had a grocery shop in the early part of the last century, which was later moved to Dunkelly West. There is a small *cill* (burial ground) at the east side.

The Townland of Enoughter West

Derivation same as Enoughter East, above. The area of the townland is 166 acres.

	Population	*Houses*
1841	70	13
1851	50	7
1997	7	5

Three houses are occupied and two are holiday homes. Tenants' names in the 1850s were Goggin, Wilkinson, Reilly and Lamb. The landlord was Margaret Notter. Nothing of historical or archaeological importance is recorded in this townland.

The Townland of Goleen

Gabhailín means 'little sea inlet'. The area of the village and townland is 58 acres.

	Population	Houses
1841	144	26
1851	117	18
1997	46	46

Twenty-six houses are occupied, three are vacant and 17 are holiday homes. Tenants' names in the 1850s were Goggin, Sullivan, King, Doran, Swanton, Murphy, Nolan, Fleming, McCarthy, Crowley, Wilbank, Donovan, Scullly, Rev John Foley, Hall Townsend, Notter and Rev Percival Myles. The landlord was Alicia Maria Notter.

The present RC church was built by Fr John Foley and opened in 1854. Goleen Protestant church (now a heritage centre) opened in 1841. The rectory nearby was built by Rev Fisher in 1880. The new medical dispensary in the village opened in 1998. There is a *cill* (burial ground) at the south side of the townland. A pound field (where cattle were impounded) was at the rear of the village, near the river. The old RIC barracks in the village was to the rear of Sheehan's public house.

Services provided and shop owners in past time were as follows: The post office was owned by N O'Sullivan in the 1930s–1950s; it was later owned by J Harrington and S Harrington, and is now run by AM O'Callaghan.

Nancy O'Sullivan had a drapery in the early twentieth century. A drapery outlet was also provided in recent times by Sean McCarthy, in addition to a public house facility. This premises is now The Fastnet, subsequently owned by the Doyle/Kingston family.

A general store and public house was owned by J McCarthy in the middle of the last century. This premises was later run by May McCarthy and is now owned by D O'Meara.

McCormicks had a hotel and bar; this premises was later owned by T Coughlan and is now owned by F Coughlan.

Dan and Ethel O'Sullivan had a grocery business. This is now the supermarket service provided by Anne Marie O'Callaghan. The old post office (O'Sullivan's) is now a grocery store owned by D Sheehan. A guest house was run by Ms Barnett; and Crowleys had a small grocery store.

Hardware stores were owned by Scully, Harrington and Mahony, who had both hardware and fish-buying businesses in the 1920s. This former business premises is now a bar owned by N Sheehan. A meat shop in past times was owned by Mahony's; currently this service is provided by T & M McCarthy. Ritchie and Liz Barry have a take-away service in the village. Shoe-making and repair facilities were provided by J O'Mahony and later by J Donovan.

Additional services provided in Goleen today are a telecommunication centre run by Mizen Vision, and a marine and cliff rescue service.

The Townland of Gortbrack

Gort Breac means 'spotted or striped field'. The area of the townland is 105 acres.

	Population	Houses
1841	53	8
1851	38	6
1997	3	4

Two houses are occupied and two are holiday homes. Tenants' names in the 1850s were Driscoll, Leary, Carty, Gallagher and Sullivan. The landlord was Rev Thomas O'Grady. Carthoge Fort was in the townland, but was demolished, possibly at the end of the nineteenth century.

The Townland of Gortduv

Gortduv or *gort dubh* means 'black field'. The area of the townland is 221 acres.

	Population	Houses
1841	131	23
1851	79	14
1997	9	9

Three houses are occupied, four are unoccupied and two are holiday homes. Tenants' names in the 1850s were Burke, Carthy, Coughlan, Downey, Colbert, Regan, McCarthy and Harnett. The landlord was Lionel J Fleming. A Church Education Society school (Protestant) opened in this townland in 1848 and closed the following year. In that year it recorded 116 pupils. A Hodnett family were masons and carpenters here in past times.

The Townland of Gortnacarriga

Gort na Carraige means 'field of rocks'. The area of the townland is 273 acres.

	Population	Houses
1841	110	20
1851	63	13
1997	20	8

Five houses are occupied and three are holiday homes. Tenants' names in the 1850s were Hart, Driscoll, Shea, Peer, Coughlan, Supple, Glavin, Lemon, Hall and Mehigan. The landlord was the Rev T O'Grady.

The Protestant school in the townland in the 1850s was vested in Rev W Fisher. The last school closed in 1926/7 when there were seven pupils on the rolls. Frances Levis was the last teacher. On closure the pupils were transported to the Altar school, as Ballydevlin school was temporarily closed. Carrigamanus House is in this townland; this was the home of the Dowe family in the seventeenth century and was later residence of the Rev Thomas O'Grady. There is a small burial ground in the townland.

The Townland of Gortnagashel

Gort na gCaiseal means 'field of the stone fort' or habitation. No trace of these remain now. The area of the townland is 80 acres.

	Population	Houses
1841	39	5
1851	16	2
1997	0	0

As with the townland of Knockatassaig, this townland has no residents or houses. Maurice Downey and Robert Allen were the only residents in the 1850s. The landlord was Rev T O'Grady. Nothing of historical or archaeological importance is recorded for this townland.

The Townland of Greenane

The Irish name *Grianan* means 'sunny place'. The area of the townland is 38 acres.

	Population	Houses
1841	38	3
1851	16	2
1997	4	2

One house is residential and one is a holiday home. The only tenant recorded in the 1850s was a Bartholomew Downey. The landlord was Lord Clinton. In recent times the remains of a mud-and-wattle hut were discovered in the townland. An old burial site here is known as 'the soldier's grave'. Also present are the remains of a *fulacht fiadh* (ancient cooking place) and some mineshafts, now backfilled.

The Townland of Gunpoint

This is one of the few townlands with an English name. In present-day Irish it is called 'Poinnte na Gunna', which is a direct translation of the English name. Possibly this townland had an old Irish name, now forgotten. It is one of the few townlands with the same name as in the 1850s.

	Population	Houses
1841	146	24
1851	66	6
1997	17	9

Six houses are occupied, one is unoccupied and two are holiday homes. Names at the time of the Griffiths Valuation list were Donovan, Callaghan, Murphy and Sullivan. The landlord was W Hull. The remains of an old stone fort are evident here, with standing stones at the entrance. At the north side, on the seafront, are the foundations of an old corn store. In these stores the corn, taken from the tenants as rent payment, was stored for export in pre-Famine and, often, in Famine times.

The Townland of Gurranes

Garráin means 'grove of thin trees'. It is 115 acres in extent.

	Population	Houses
1841	76	11
1851	63	11
1997	1	3

One house is occupied full time and two are holiday homes. Tenants' names in the 1850s were Sullivan, Donovan, Kilty, Connell and

Minihan. The landlord was William Hull. Of geological interest here are some rock surfaces with deep circular indentations.

The Townland of Gurtyowen

Gort Tighe Eoghain means 'field of Owen's house'. Its area is 259 acres.

	Population	Houses
1841	97	15
1851	94	16
1997	18	7

Five are occupied, one is unoccupied and one is a holiday home. The tenants' names in the 1850s were Mahony, Cronin, Driscoll, Leader and Daly. The landlord was the Rev WA Fisher. Connells had a grocery shop here which closed in the 1950s. A *fulacht fiadh* is at the north side of the townland.

The Townland of Kealfadda

Caol Fada literally means the 'long narrow'. It possibly refers to a stream or rocky ridge. The area of the townland is 477 acres.

	Population	Houses
1841	230	41
1851	100	16
1997	13	10

Five houses are occupied, two are unoccupied and three are holiday homes. Tenants' names in the 1850s were Connell, Hall, Coughlan, Butler, Browne, Collins, Love and Donovan. The landlord was George Bird. No archaeological or historical sites are recorded in that townland.

The Townland of Kilbarry

Cill Barra means 'church or oratory of Finbarr'. The area of the townland is 79 acres.

	Population	Houses
1841	27	3
1851	15	2
1997	0	0

Some old house ruins are now being restored. Only one tenant was recorded in the 1850s; he was Richard Connell. The landlord was

Margaret Notter. A *cill* at the top of the hill has several grave markers and a small rectangular foundation, possibly that of a little church or oratory. A second *cill* was near the main road, but no trace of this now remains. Some 19th-century mineshafts from which copper was extracted are in the townland. The remains of a large *fulacht fiadh* were discovered during recent land reclamation.

The Townland of Kilbrown

Cill Bróin meaning 'Bróin's church or oratory'. The area of the townland is 191 acres.

	Population	Houses
1841	58	9
1851	35	8
1997	15	8

Six houses are occupied and two are holiday homes. Tenants' names in the 1850s were Sheehan, Mahony, Goggin and Connor. The landlord was Lionel Fleming. Near the east side are the ruins of Kilbrown Church. This early christian site also has a burial ground, a holy well – 'tobar Bróin' – and a *baulán* stone. Near the south side is a small fort (Lisheen na Cortha) enclosed by a fosse. In the centre of the fort is a stone-lined cistern. Sheehan's had a grocery business in Kilbrown which flourished up to the 1960s.

The Townland of Kilcomane

The name comes from *Cill Damhain*, meaning 'church of St. Daman'. The area has 426 acres.

	Population	Houses
1841	196	34
1851	62	10
1997	1	4

One house is occupied, one is unoccupied and two are holiday homes. Tenants' names in the 1850s were Driscoll, Crowley, Donohoe, Hayes, Minihane, Goggin and Barry. The landlord was J O'Connell. An old burial ground is at the north-west side. This burial ground has a number of gravemarkers, including one large cross-inscribed stone. The rectangular ruins of a church were present in the nineteenth century, but are gone now.

A small pier, at the north side, was built in the 1930s to facilitate local fishermen. A pound field was in use here in the nineteenth century. At the south side is a ruin known as the burned house. From this holding Garrett Barry and his family were evicted in the early part of the last century by Bird, the landlord's agent, and his house was burned down. Today this solitary ruin is a grim reminder of past injustice. Bishop Minihane, USA, who died some years ago, had close links with this area, as his family came from this townland.

The Townland of Killeane

Cill Liadhain means 'Liadhain's Church'. Liadhain was reputed to be the mother of St Kieran of Cape Clear and had a small oratory or church here. The area of the townland is 102 acres.

	Population	Houses
1841	68	10
1851	30	6
1997	2	6

Two houses are residential, one is vacant and two are holiday homes. Coughlan and Downey were the only tenants' names listed in the 1850s. The landlord was Henry Newman. In recent times, the *cill* at the east side was destroyed during building work. In past times, a small burial ground was also at the west side.

The Townland of Kilpatrick

The name comes from *Cill Padraig*, meaning 'Patrick's church'.

	Population	Houses
1841	78	10
1851	44	6
1997	0	1

Three Reacroft families were tenants in the 1850s. The landlord was W Hull. At the south-west side of the townland is a small burial ground.

The Townland of Knock

Cnoc means 'hill'.

	Population	Houses
1841	109	17
1851	39	12
1997	10	5

There are two houses occupied and two holiday homes. Names here in the 1850s were Goggin, Coughlan, Graham, Murphy and Brown. The landlord was W Hull. The signal tower (Leamcon Tower) is in Knock townland. It was built in the early nineteenth century as part of the coastal defence system. It is now a residence.

The Townland of Knockatassaig

Cnoc a tSasanaig means 'hill of the Englishman'. The area of the townland is 94 acres.

	Population	Houses
1841	0	0
1851	1	3
1997	0	0

This is the first townland in the parish where there are no houses and no one resides (the second being Gornagashel). The following were joint users of the mountain land in the 1850s: Driscoll, Leary, Carty, Gallagher, Sullivan, Regan, Simmons, Mahony, Rev Fisher, Daly and Love. The landlord was Rev T O'Grady. On top of the hill is a cross inscribed on the rockface; the dating is uncertain. Some ruined huts are also on the hillside and an enclosure with a boundary wall.

The Townland of Knockeenageragh

Cnuicin na gCaorach means 'small hill of the sheep'. The area of the townland is 126 acres.

	Population	Houses
1841	65	10
1851	19	3
1997	1	5

One house is occupied, one is unoccupied and three are holiday homes. Tenants' names in the 1850s were Downey, Coughlan, Barry, McCormack, Sullivan and Gleeson. The landlord was Lord Clinton. Goleen creamery is in the townland, opened in June 1959; it was replaced by the 'travelling creamery'. D O'Sullivan was the first creamery manager.

The Townland of Knockeens

Cnuicíní means 'small hills'. Its area is 228 acres.

	Population	Houses
1841	123	19
1851	81	12
1997	12	9

Seven houses are occupied and two are holiday homes. Tenants' names in the 1850s were McCarthy, Mahony, Evans, Murphy, Driscoll, Twomey, Hitchcock and Murray. The landlord was James O'Callaghan. Jeremiah Murray had a forge here in the 1850s.

A shoemaker also plied his trade here in the nineteenth century, but his name is now unknown. A cliff-edge fort is at the west end, and is now partly eroded. This place is believed to be the original foundation of the O'Mahony Castle, which was subsequently built across the bay in Dunmanus.

The Townland of Knocknagullane

Cnoc a'Ghallain means 'hill of the standing stones'. The area of this townland is 118 acres.

	Population	Houses
1841	51	10
1851	36	6
1997	7	5

Two houses are residential and three are holiday homes. Tenants' names in the 1850s were Barry, Murphy, Mahony and Driscoll. The landlord was Lord Clinton. The *galáns* or standing stones that were in the townland are now gone. Steve Barry had a shoe-making and repair facility here early in the twentieth century.

The Townland of Lackareagh

Leaca Riabhach means 'grey sloping area'. Its area is 326 acres.

	Population	Houses
1841	78	12
1851	52	5
1997	6	3

Two houses are occupied and one is unoccupied. Only one tenant's name is recorded in the 1850s: Minihane. The landlord was G Swanton.

The Townland of Lackavaun

Lackavaun or *Leaca Bhan* means 'white sloping hillside'. The area of the townland is 226 acres.

	Population	*Houses*
1841	85	17
1851	66	14
1997	8	7

Three houses are occupied and four are holiday homes. Tenants' names in the 1850s were Reilly, Hegarty, Coughlan, Donovan, Sullivan, Long, Murphy, Sweeney, Burchill, Reacroft. The landlord was Mr Uniake. A slate quarry was worked in the townland in the nineteenth century.

The Townland of Lackenakea

Leacan Mhic Aodha means the hillside of the son of Aodha. Its area is 112 acres.

	Population	*Houses*
1841	34	6
1851	20	4
1997	5	2

One house is residential and one is a holiday home. Tenants' names in the 1850s were Love, Hegarty and Sullivan. The landlord was William Levis. A caravan site is in the townland where hundreds of holiday makers stay in the summer. Glanville's had a grocery shop here early in the nineteenth century.

The Townland of Leamcon

Leimcon is the Irish for 'hound's leap'. There are, however, other interpretations of this name. It has an area of 136 acres.

	Population	*Houses*
1841	82	12
1851	33	7
1997	17	7

Four houses are occupied, two are holiday homes and one is unoccupied. Tenants' names in the 1850s were Hull, Reacroft, Lannon and Dawley (gate lodge). The landlord was W Hull. Leamcon House was the residence of the Hull family – landlords of this district for almost

300 years. Many aspects of the colonial period are still visible: walled gardens and fields, stone-lined wells, ruined battery, etc. Archaeological sites include a castle site, henge fort and the site of Kilmurray church and graveyard. A Church Education Society (Protestant) opened here in the late 1840s, largely for the purpose of prosletysing. The highest number of pupils recorded was 141 in 1847. An earlier Catholic school functioned here in pre-Famine times. This would have been called a hedge school, though sometimes it was actually a mud hut. A rural shop functioned here from the 1920s to the 1980s; owned by Cowhigs and later by Mary Regan. Court sessions were held at Leamcon House, by William Hull, magistrate.

The Townland of Leenane

Lionan means 'shallow area where seaweed abounds'. The area of the townland is 95 acres.

	Population	Houses
1841	132	27
1851	52	13
1997	3	8

One house is residential and seven are holiday homes. The ruined remains of a fish palace is on the seafront. Pilchards abounded off the coast in the seventeenth century. The fish were dried after the oil was extracted at the fish palace. The oil was used as a lubricant for guns, etc.

A pier used by fishing vessels and holiday makers is nearby. At the south east is a megalithic tomb of a type known as a wedge grave, dating from 2000 BC. This is known locally as 'King's Grave'. These tombs were used for both inhumation and cremated burials.

Tessings had a grocery shop here in the 1930s–1940s and also a shoe-making and repair facility for a short period. In the townland also an open-air dance platform provided for the social needs of the area in the 1940s–1950s.

The Townland of Letter

Leitir means 'wet hillside'. The area of the townland is 219 acres.

	Population	Houses
1841	134	21
1851	50	10
1997	15	9

Six houses are residential and three are holiday homes. Tenants' names in the 1850s were Downey, Mahony, Collins and Driscolls. The landlord was Henry E Warren. On Letter hill is a small stone circle with a cross-inscribed stone. Local tradition says this is the burial place of Liadhain, mother of St Kieran. Nearby is a holy well known as 'Tobarilla' (*tobar ula*) – 'well of the pentitential rounds' – where rounds were made in the recent past on the eve of St John's Day, 23rd/24th June.

A print on a rock on the hill is known as the priest's footprint. A place on the north side is called Shanamullin. The name suggests a mill was possibly sited here on the river. Slate was quarried on Letter hill in the last century. A Kelly family had a grocery shop here at the turn of the century and a *shebeen* was in the townland in past times. A large *fulacht fiadh* (ancient cooking place) complete with cooking troughs, was also in the townland, but was removed in the 1930s–1940s. The forge owned by Hourihan at the north side was in use early in the twentieth century. This was known as Letter forge, but is in the townland of Ballyvogue Beg.

The Townland of Lissacaha

'*Lios a'Caha*' means 'the fort of the battle'. It is 779 acres in area.

	Population	Houses
1841	281	41
1851	154	25
1997	29	20

Fourteen houses are occupied, three are unoccupied and three are holiday homes. Tenants' names in the 1850s were Reacroft, Hegarty, Houlihan, Notter, Mahony, Lannan, Attridge, Skuce, Sweetnam, Slatter, Carthy, Johnson, Camierie, Regan and Hurley. The landlord was Richard Notter.

Ancient sites include a triple-fossed ring fort – the largest in West Cork – and a *galán* at the east side. Evidence of a *fulacht fiadh* (ancient cooking place) was found at the north side during recent land reclamation. A pound field was at the east side in the nineteenth century.

The Church of Ireland school, which opened in 1845, closed in 1985. A pupil roll of 174 was recorded in its first year. At the time of closure there was only one pupil in the roll book. The small Methodist church built in 1930 is used occasionally for worship. This church replaced an earlier preaching house, which was further east.

The Swanton family owned a grocery shop which closed in the recent past. The Hegarty family operated a smithy in the early part of the last century. The O'Driscolls also had a forge here for a short while. Lissacaha Cottage at the south side was the home of Richard Notter, landlord.

The Townland of Lissacaha North

Lios a'Chatha Thuaidh is a separate townland, distinct from Lissacaha (fort of the battle). It is 346 acres in size.

	Population	Houses
1841	100	14
1851	43	8
1997	23	10

Eight houses are occupied, one is unoccupied and one is a holiday home. In Griffiths Valuation list, Philip Somerville was the landlord and the only occupier of land in Lissacaha North. He lived in the Prarie Cottages. John Gillivan lived in a rented house in the townland. Part of the townland is known as the Prarie – so named by Mr Somerville. The old name for the north side is Maulnacarriga and the south side was known as Meall a'Mhadra. The old RIC barracks was at the west side. A Logan family had a grocery shop there in the early part of the last century.

The Townland of Lissagriffin

Lios Ui Criomhthain means 'Griffin's fort'. Another interpretation gives the name as 'fort of the foxes' – *criomhthain* being an old Irish name for foxes. The area of the townland is 345 acres.

	Population	Houses
1841	236	34
1851	84	16
1997	26	18

Tenants' names in the 1850s were Glavin, Cotter, Driscoll, Broghan, Carty, Mahony, Meade, Reilly, Sullivan, Harrington, Driscoll, Leary and the Rev Fisher. The landlord was Lord Clinton.

Many sites of archaeological and historical importance are in the townland. These include the ancient church ruin of Kilmoe and its adjoining cemetery, the large *baulán* stone near the entrance to the graveyard and the nearby rock surface decorated with ancient rock art. The site of a castle is in the townland. This was one of the 15th-century O'Mahony castles in the Mizen peninsula. No trace of the castle now remains. There are a number of standing stones at the north and west sides. The remains of a ring fort are also here. This is possibly the fort that gives its name to the townland. An earthern work of uncertain origin is at the west side, and a small burial ground is nearby.

Lissagriffin has a long tradition of national school education. The first school was opened in 1849 by Fr John Foley, with 78 pupils on the rolls. Jeremiah Cronin was the first national school teacher. Before the days of the national school, a man named Hodnett taught in a hedge school in the townland. The national school was rebuilt in 1882 and served the area until closure in 1958, when a new two-teacher school was opened further west. This school now has 25 pupils on its roll (1997) and is the only rural school in the parish.

In the nineteenth century a pound field was in use in the townland. Community services early in the last century were supplied by Mahony's grocery shop, Harrington's forge and Driscoll's shoemaker shop.

The Townland of Lowertown

	Population	Houses
1841	342	62
1851	171	29
1997	55	33

Seventeen houses are occupied today, three unoccupied and thirteen are holiday homes. Tenants' names listed here in the 1850s (Griffiths Valuation) were Moynihan, Foran, McCarthy, Pyburn, Levis, Mahony, Cole, Attridge, Camiere, Driscoll, Daly, Barnett, and Rev J Foley. The landlord was W Hull. At the west side of the townland is a burial ground known as the 'cill', where the last burial took place in the 1940s. In the centre is Rath Amhlaibh, a large Iron Age ring fort. At the south side is a mass rock in a secluded glen. On the seafront was a large grain store, which was demolished for roadmaking in the 1940s. This stone was used in Famine times as a fever hospital and auxillary workhouse. Some copper mining was also done in this townland in the last century. On the north side of the main road are the ruins of the old post office, owned by the McLean family. It functioned up to the 1920s. Lowertown Lodge was the seat of JB Fleming, the landlord's agent for that district. Callaghan's shop, one of the rapidly disappearing rural shops, was the home of Mikie Callaghan, the last shoemaker to function in the parish. Nearby on the riverbank was a smithy owned by P Hegarty. The site of this forge is now part of the car park for Lowertown Church.

The Townland of Mallavogue

Meal Ui Bhuadaigh means 'mound or small hill of O'Bogue'. The area of the townland is 254 acres.

	Population	Houses
1841	108	16
1851	54	14
1997	0	2

Both houses are holiday homes. Tenants' names in the 1850s (Griffiths Valuation) were McCarthy, Sullivan, Mahony, Leary, Harris and the Browhead Mining Company. The landlord was Lord Clinton. The west point of the townland is known as Brow Head: *bro* was the old Irish word for quern stones. Possibly quern stones were quarried at Brow Head in past times.

On Brow Head also stands a 19th-century signal tower. These towers were part of the coastal defence system at that time. A Marconi wireless transmitting station was built on the head early in the last century. This station was used by the military during World War I, and was burned down by the Irish Republican Army in 1922, during the War of Independence. Copper mines were extensively worked here in the nineteenth century. Some of the mineshafts extended outwards under the sea bed. Slate was also quarried at the cliff face near the south side.

The Townland of Mauladinna

Meáll a'Deanna means 'hill of the view'. It is 319 acres in extent.

	Population	Houses
1841	90	16
1851	55	9
1997	2	3

The one house is occupied and one is a holiday home. Tenants' names in the 1850s were Luacey, Cronin, Hickey, Sweeney, Dawley, Harnett, Ellis and Hurley. The landlords were W Baldwin and A O'Driscoll.

The Townland of Oughminna (Oughtminee)

Ucht Mine means 'hill breast of the plain'. The area of the townland is 167 acres.

	Population	Houses
1841	56	10
1851	38	7
1997	3	3

One house is occupied, one is unoccupied and one is a holiday home. Tenants' names in the 1850s were Sheehan, McCarthy, Leahy, Coughlan, Leary and Cody. The landlord was the Rev T O'Grady.

The Townland of Rathooragh

Rath Tuarta means 'fort of the paddocks'. Another interpretation is *Rath Teamhrach*' meaning 'prominent fort'. This is the largest town-land in the parish, containing 1,183 acres.

	Population	Houses
1841	381	65
1851	163	29
1997	23	16

Nine houses are occupied and seven are unoccupied. Tenants' names in the 1850s were Burke, Foley, Mahony, Hegarty, Minihane, Ellis, Driscoll, McCarthy, O'Brien, Cotter, Lucey, Sullivan, Reacroft and Roberts. Landlords were Richard Beecher and William Preston White.

Two souterrains (underground passages) are in the townland – one, stone-lined, at the west, and another discovered during land reclamation further east. A number of *fulacht fiadhs* (ancient cooking places) were also discovered here recently. The Stone Age fort, from which the townland derives its name, is in the centre. In the early part of the nineteenth century a Driscoll family owned a *shebeen* here. A forge was in the townland but the name is now unknown. A field known as the tailor's field, suggests a tailor also lived here in past times.

The Townland of Rock Island

This is another one of the few townlands with an English name. The Irish version is *Oileán na Carraige*. The area of the townland is 61 acres.

	Population	Houses
1841	119	22
1851	111	24
1997	8	11

Eight are holiday homes and three are residential. In addition the old coastguard station is now converted to flats. The tenants' names in the 1850s were Evans, Applethorne, Ducket, Hill, Goodfellow, Webb, Thomas, Matthews, Baker, Capithorn, Roe, Barry, Mahony, Sheehan, Hamilton and Downey. The landlord was Thomas Notter. In the Tithe Allotments (1822), part of the townland was known as Gurteen.

In the 1840s the island had a post office, where Rick Hamilton was postmaster in the 1860s–1870s, and a dispensary, owned by Dr McCormack. A Church Education Society school opened in Famine times. It had 85 pupils on its rolls in 1848. Mr Baker taught in the school in the 1850s. A lighthouse was built in the 1840s, and also in the nineteenth century a boat industry flourished at Cuas na mhairt.

Prior to the Griffith road to Crookhaven being built, a ferry operated between the island and Crookhaven. Rock Island House was built by the Notters in the seventeenth century. The pilotage towers on the island and in Crookhaven were built by the Notters and Coughlans in the nineteenth century. They were used as navigational aids when Crookhaven was a major port of call for transatlantic shipping. (The Crookhaven towers are now gone.)

In recent times a thriving lobster industry flourished in Rock Island. Owned by a French company, its local representatives were Rickard Collins and Sonny O'Sullivan. A small industry (Cottage Foods) owned by Tony Fitzgibbon now uses the premises to produce garlic butter. The old coastguard station (now rebuilt) was burned down during the War of Independence, 1921–1922.

The Townland of Shanavalley

Sean Bhaile means 'old hamlet or place of habitation'. The area of the townland is 85 acres.

	Population	Houses
1841	63	12
1851	45	12
1997	6	2

One house is residential and one is a holiday home. Tenants' names in the 1850s were Burchill, Driscoll, Gallagher, Lamb, Mahony, Thomas,

Field, Sheehan, Hamilton and Notter. The landlord was Thomas Notter. In the 1850 Griffiths Valuation, Thomas Field was owner of a house and orchards now owned by the Doyle/Kingston family.

Michael Harrington, who served his country by joining the Fenian movement in 1867–68, had close association with this townland. As a young man when working as a boat builder on Rock Island, he carved his name on the rockface at the west end of Shanavalley. This inscription is still in pristine condition.

Harrington was later arrested in Dublin, convicted as a Fenian felon and deported to the penal colony of Freemantle, Australia. He was rescued with other convicts in 1876 by Captain Anthony of the whaler *Catalpa* in what was one of the most dramatic and daring rescues ever effected.

The Townland of Spanish Cove

This is an English name, Gaelicised to *Cuas na Spainneach*. The area of the townland is 84 acres.

	Population	Houses
1841	80	14
1851	61	13
1997	3	9

Seven houses are holiday homes and two are residential. Tenants' names in the 1850s were Driscoll, Barnane, Notter, Mahony, Coughlan and McCormack. The landlord was Thomas Notter. A small foundation, possibly of a tower, is at the east side.

In the 1850s a company was formed to mine for copper in Spanish Cove; it was subsequently known as the Spanish Cove Bubble Company. Former Attorney General and EU Commissioner, Peter Sutherland, has a residence in the townland.

The Townland of Toor

Tuar means 'bleach area' (wool or flax). The area of the townland is 213 acres.

	Population	Houses
1841	50	9
1851	32	4
1997	2	4

One house is occupied and three are holiday homes. Tenants' names in the 1850s were Coughlan and Burchill. The landlord was the Rev T

O'Grady. At the north side is Toor pier, much frequented by rod fishermen.

The Townland of Toormore

Toor Mor means 'large bleach field'; possibly used for wool bleaching. The area of the townland is 601 acres.

	Population	Houses
1841	370	73
1851	343	71
1997	39	41

Eighteen houses are occupied, three are unoccupied and 20 are holiday homes. Tenants' names in the 1850s were Bayley, Bridge, Pyburn, Barry, Melville, Johnson, Mahony, Coughlan, Neville, Bennett, Hegarty, Sullivan, Allen, Glanville, Mehigan, Donovan, Redcroft, Ferguson, Horgan, Cunningham, Geaney and Rev E Hopley. The landlord was Rev WA Fisher.

Archaeologcal sites include a Bronze Age wedge tomb. This was recently excavated when, among other artefacts, a Bronze Age axe was discovered. A *baulán* stone is near the east side and some old copper mine workings further north. Toormore was a hive of industry in times past where trades and tradesmen abounded and several shops flourished. In the 1850s a Daniel Donovan had a smithy here and William Allen had a tailor's shop. A forge was also owned by the Sullivans in the early part of the nineteenth century. The Pyburns were both carpenters and boat builders, and Cullinane had a carpenter's shop on an island offshore. R Jermyn and J Cotter were masons, Cunningham had a shoemaker shop, and a dressmaker also worked here in the 1930s. T Jermyn had a milling business in the 1930s–1940s.

Rural shops were owned at various times by Allen's, Mrs Donovan, Bennett's, Barry's and Jermyn's. Jermyn's shop is one of the two privately owned rural shops in the parish that still functions. Toormore Post Office also operates from this premises. During the 1940s–1970s the post office was at the east side and run by Ted O'Sullivan. The old rectory was at the south side and is now a private residence.

In the 1800s, court sessions were held in the townland in Baylie's office. National schools for both boys and girls were opened by Fr Foley in 1849. The number of pupils recorded in 1852 was 165 boys and 158 girls. Denis Hegarty was one of the teachers. A hedge school operated in pre-Famine times and a Mr Burke was the master. A secluded area at the east side is known as Glantan.

The Townland of Toureen

Tuarín means 'small bleach area', where wool or flax was bleached. The area of the townland is 122 acres.

	Population	Houses
1841	50	12
1851	12	4
1997	0	3

Two houses are unoccupied and one is a holiday home. Driscoll and Donovan were the tenants' names in the *Valuation of Tenements* in the 1850s. The landlord was Lord Clinton. A megalithic tomb (wedge grave) is at the north-west side and a large stone with cup marks is in the centre of the townland.

The Brow Head stone quarry is in the townland. It is known locally as the 'Granny Quarry' – so named from Granny Island off shore. The stone from the quarry was hard grey-green sandstone, sometimes mistakenly called granite, which is non-existent in the Mizen peninsula. The quarry opened in the 1920s and closed in 1939. During that period thousands of tons of stone was quarried, crushed on site and exported to England. A large local labour force was employed for this work.

Credits

Goleen townland was the final townland in the parish series. The first issue opened in the Parish Newsletter on 20th April 1997 – two years ago. Throughout the series I have endeavoured to co-ordinate the various aspects of local history and past times of each townland. Doubtless there were some omissions due to lack of information, and, as I said at the outset, some townland history many be displaced due to difficulty in identifying boundaries. My grateful thanks to Fr Cashman for his co-operation and patience in deciphering my often times hastily written notes; and to Tara O'Sullivan, who sometimes had the task of getting them on to computer. The following were most helpful with information on their own areas as we moved along: Jim McGrath, Michael Collins, Mary Walsh, Bridie Kennedy, Eileen Scully, George Harnedy, Con and Mary Lucey, Declan O'Mahony, Pat McCarthy, Betty Barry, Tess Cullinane, Angela O'Donovan, Rose O'Sullivan, Joe Hurley, Dan O'Leary, Timmy and Mary O'Sullivan, Richard Lannin NT, John Wilcox, Gerry and Eileen Coughlan, Denis Downey, Denis and Mar Donovan, Jimmy Newman, Jack O'Driscoll,

Michael McCarthy, Anthony O'Callaghan, Jack O'Sullivan, Eugene Downing, Maggie (Batt) Downey, Florence O'Driscoll, Connie O'Donovan and C Sullivan. Goleen Parish has a rich cultural and historical past. I hope you enjoyed our journey through it.

– Michael R O'Donovan

Thank you, Michael Raymond

Reading the credits made me aware of the enormous amount of work involved in consultation, discerning boundaries, etc., as well as consulting historical and archaeological sources. The present and future parishioners are deeply indebted to Michael. We know he is busy in so many other projects of this nature after his days farming. Lesser mortals would have said, 'Sorry – no time!' I thoroughly enjoyed getting this information every week and know it was the number one read in the Newsletter for locals and visitors alike. I notice that some of the people thanked have gone to their eternal reward recently. RIP. The wisdom of the elderly is fast disappearing. Thanks be to God, and to all concerned, for what was preserved in the series on the parish townlands.

– Denis J Cashman, PP

Sadly, since the above tribute was paid to Michael Raymond O'Donovan, he too passed to his eternal reward on 13th April 2003. *Go Raibh Deis De ar a Anam.*